WORKING WITH DANES

TIPS FOR AMERICANS

KAY XANDER MELLISH

Forlag: BoD – Books on Demand, København, Danmark
Tryk: BoD – Books on Demand, Norderstedt, Tyskland
ISBN: 978-87-4302-813-0

For June 5 and September 17

Introduction

If you're an American who is about to do business in Denmark, the Danes you meet will probably know a lot more about your country than you do about theirs.

US movies, TV, and streaming services are all popular in Denmark, and Danes also like US music and fashion. Some have passionate opinions about US politics. Many Danes have visited the US or even spent an exchange year there during high school.

On the other hand, if Americans hear about Denmark at all, they often hear information that is not entirely correct.

For example, Denmark is not "socialist" – it's a social welfare state, a free-market economy in which the voters have agreed to be taxed very highly in exchange for universal health care and tuition-free universities.

(Anyone who shops in a Danish supermarket will get a sense of what the national 25% sales tax does to the price of groceries.)

Denmark also isn't the cheerful utopia some people on the left would like it to be.

Everyone must work and pay taxes to keep the welfare state financed. And social services are closely measured and monitored to keep people from riding for free.

The country has some of the toughest immigration

rules in Europe, rules that have forced many well-meaning Americans out of the country, including some married to Danes.

Fewer people than Houston

Denmark is *small*. With fewer than six million people, it has a lower population than metropolitan Houston.

Yet because of its high educational levels and long history as a trading nation, it still produces regular innovations in pharmaceuticals, engineering, and green technology, not to mention world-famous Danish design.

Having lived and worked in both the US and Denmark, I have a great fondness for both countries. I hope you'll enjoy working in Denmark and with the Danes.

Kay Xander Mellish
Copenhagen, Fall 2020

Why Denmark is a great place to do business

Denmark is a lovely, quiet, gentle country with well-educated people who speak excellent English.

Infrastructure is superb, with well-paved roads and buses and trains that run mostly on time. Internet access is almost universal, and digital initiatives have made the Danish government largely paperless.

Corruption is minimal[1], a key factor in persuading the populace to pay some of the world's highest taxes.

It's less upsetting to see a substantial chunk disappear from your salary when you believe the funds are being used for roads, schools, and hospitals, not to line some corrupt politician's pockets.

---

1   *Denmark is one of the world's least corrupt countries, according to Transparency International's 2019 Corruption Perception Index.*

Employee relations

The tax system in Denmark is much more transparent than the US system, and legal systems in general tend to be simpler and easier to understand.

So are the rules about working conditions. Maximum working hours, required vacations, and termination procedures for salaried employees are outlined in a national law that every corporate HR person knows backwards.

Conditions for hourly employees generally follow rules outlined by their unions, who make umbrella agreements with the companies in their sector.

Unions are also the first touchpoint when it comes to employee disputes, even for knowledge-sector employees.

That means less running back and forth to HR. And wrongful termination suits and discrimination filings are less common in Denmark than they are in the US.

In general, Denmark is much less litigious, which means much less record-keeping and monitoring is required.

Work-life balance

Denmark is known for its work-life balance, which applies to managers as well as their teams.

Most Danish offices are empty by 4pm, as both male and female employees rush home to pick up their children and prepare a fresh dinner. (They often log on again after the kids are in bed to finish up assignments.)

Time off is sacred in Denmark: full-time workers get a minimum of five weeks' vacation per year and usually take two to three weeks in a row during the summer.

Many companies close down entirely during the last two weeks of July and between Christmas and New Year's.

If you choose to stay in the office at this time, you'll find there's not much to do besides tidy your desk or make plans for busier times ahead.

"Merchant Harbor"

Although its emphasis on a well-rounded life is part of its appeal, Denmark is a place that respects business.

The name *Copenhagen*, the country's capital and largest city, translates literally to "merchant's harbor."

For hundreds of years, ships have been sailing in and out with goods and people under the flag of trade.

If you're just arriving to do business in Denmark, you're the newest thread in the centuries-old tapestry of Danish commerce. Welcome.

Two words to better understand your Danish colleagues

Two words that will help you understand your Danish colleagues both begin with A, and you will see a lot of them in this book.

The first is *authenticity*. Danes have a visceral dislike for anyone or anything who pretends to be something they're not.

This will apply to you when job hunting or on the job – don't exaggerate your capabilities or promise influence you don't have – and to your products.

The concept of overselling your product, or promoting features that are perhaps not entirely proven yet, is totally unacceptable to the Danes.

Danish business, like Danish society, is based on trust.

Trust is usually given by default, but if you lose your credibility it will be almost impossible to get it back.

Dislike of authority

The second is *anti-authoritarianism*.

This is a society that has an intense dislike for authority and elites.

Advanced programs for "gifted children" are rare; instead, talented kids are expected to help their struggling classmates.

A degree from a prestigious university is also not the crucial differentiator that it is in the US. There are only eight universities in Denmark, all of them excellent.

In the workplace, everyone gets to have their say, even the most junior employees.

Don't show up in Denmark expecting automatic respect based on your title, your position, or your academic credentials.

Acting like visiting royalty is a sure way to antagonize the Danes.

Better to be friendly, humble, and down-to-earth — which is how the real-life Danish Royal Family conducts itself.

The sacred value of time

Nothing is more sacred to a Dane than their time.

Danes value time more than they value money or prestige. What they want to use that time on is up to them: family, hobbies, or the unquenchable Danish passion for fixing up their homes.

Never waste a Dane's time. Someone who is tardy is seen to be untrustworthy, which is why it's important to never be late to either a social appointment or a business meeting.

A 10am meeting really is a 10am meeting – not a 10:05 meeting. 10am sharp. (Americans sometimes unconsciously arrive late to show how busy and important they are. *Sorry I'm late! I was on the phone with the President.*)

Also, a little friendly chatter before getting down to business is fine, but keep it short.

In general, the Danes prefer to work first and socialize later.

Taking time off work

In the US, taking time off work can be seen as a little selfish, as if you're not really doing your part for the team.

But for Danes, one of the main purposes of work is to finance one's time off. They will take every single day of their allotted vacation time, often at their bosses' insistence.

If they're at all sick, they will stay home, and disturbing them (even if you have an angry customer on the line) is simply not done.

Most companies also allow parents to take a day or two off to care for a sick child, and Danish law provides for extensive parental leave when a child is born or adopted.

Some companies will hire a specific "parental leave cover" person for the nine to twelve months a staffer will be away.

There's no point in bothering a Danish colleague on parental leave. They usually have no idea what's going on back at the office, and they like it that way.

Job-switching is common

On a macro level, Danes don't want to waste time doing a job they don't enjoy.

Job switching is common – employees in Denmark

change jobs more often than in any other country in Europe[1] – and the small size of the Danish market means your best employees have plenty of contacts among your competitors.

That's why it's vital to make sure your Danish employees feel engaged and challenged on the job.

They won't stay with your company purely out of fear, because the Danish social system gives them a soft pillow to fall on.

Work must have meaning

You also won't make Danes happier just by giving them a glittering job title.

Even a raise, while appreciated, will mostly vanish into the jaws of the tax department.

To keep good Danish employees, you'll have to make them feel that their work has meaning and that their contribution is valued.

God arbejdslyst! is an age-old phrase you'll sometimes hear Danes saying to each other as they embark on a project.

It translates to, "Enjoy your work!"

---

1   *According to 2018 statistics from Eurostat, the EU's statistical bureau, 11.8% of Danes age 25-64 changed jobs in the previous year. In nearby Sweden, the rate was 6.2%.*

Danish names

Looking up your Danish colleagues' names in a directory can be a little tricky if you don't know the inside rules of Danish names.

A large percentage of your colleagues will have similar last names – Hansen, Nielsen, Jensen. These are old composites meaning "son of Hans", "son of Niels", and "son of Jens".

Trying to distinguish between so many people with the same name is as frustrating for the Danes as it is for you, particularly since many people also have similar first names.

If you're searching for someone called Niels Jensen or Jens Nielsen on LinkedIn, the Danes' favorite social media network, you'll find dozens of people named precisely the same thing.

Note the middle name

That's why it's key to focus on the middle name – say, Niels *Smedegaard* Jensen. These family names often mean a lot to the Danes, since they harken back to a special farm (*gaard*=farm) that may be in the living memory of older relatives.

For that reason, you may find Danish colleagues referring to the man you know as Niels Jensen as *Niels Smedegaard*, particularly if there is another Niels Jensen on the payroll. After work when they are sharing a beer, they may even just call him *Smedegaard*.

Women and names

Danish women sometimes take their partner's name when they marry, and sometimes don't. (And they often do not marry at all; it's common to have long partnerships and several children without the benefit of a ceremony.)

At any rate, you're spared the worry about whether to call someone Miss, Mrs., or Ms., since these terms have almost entirely died out in Denmark, except on airplane tickets.

If you're addressing communication to a Danish woman, just use her full name: *Anne-Sophie Mølgaard Nielsen*.

Should you need to distinguish her from another woman with a similar name, you can add her occupation up front: *IT Specialist Anne-Sophie Mølgaard Nielsen*.

Extra letters in the alphabet

Danish has three letters that don't exist in English: Æ, Ø, and Å. They are placed at the very end of the alphabet, which is why you'll find any word beginning with these letters at the back of the dictionary.

Æ can be replaced with AE and Ø with OE if you lack a Danish keyboard.

Å is sometimes replaced with the double-letter A: the large city of Århus even officially changed its name to Aarhus to make it easier for internationals to type.

The Danish "flat hierarchy"

If you ask the Danes what they like about their business culture, they're sure to mention the *flat hierarchy*.

What they mean is that a management pyramid that might have ten or more layers in a hierarchical country like Japan has only two or three layers in Denmark.

The flat hierarchy is a virtue born of necessity: salaries are high in Denmark, so middle managers are expensive.

And because Danes aren't supervised or monitored as much as Americans, middle management isn't as necessary.

Just ordinary guys and gals

With so few layers, the opportunities for promotion and a better title are slim, which can be kind of a drag if you're the sort of person who is motivated by advancement.

In fact, to admit that there's any hierarchy at all is somewhat embarrassing to the anti-authoritarian Danes.

This is why top managers will go out of their way to show they are just ordinary guys and gals, carefully putting their coffee cup in the dishwasher after the team breakfast.

And when it's time for yet another company boozefest, the big boss is expected to drink and dance right alongside everyone else.

Talking to top management

This presumed access to top management also means that employees may want to share their thoughts directly with the big boss.

One local head of a US Fortune 500 company told me that his Danish employees were driving him crazy.

"Whenever they have an idea, they come straight to me," he said. "I tell them: You've got a direct supervisor, talk to that person. I can't keep track of input from almost 200 people."

The flat hierarchy and loneliness

One aspect of the flat hierarchy that isn't always discussed is that it can lead to silo thinking and loneliness.

The hierarchy is so pared-down that each employee is doing something different, and nobody really knows what anyone else is doing.

The skeleton crew supervising them are so busy themselves that they don't have time to monitor everything their team is up to.

And so the silo'ed employee works on, unsure if what she is doing is really vital to the company's mission or if it is just *pseudo work*[1], the topic of a wildly popular book about Danish office life.

---

1   *Pseudoarbejde, by Anders Fogh Jensen and Dennis Nørmark*

Flexicurity and unions

Another word you may hear when Danish business culture is discussed is *flexicurity*, a combination of "flexible" and "security".

This means that in Denmark it's relatively easy to hire and fire employees, but the social welfare system gives them a soft cushion to fall back on.

Litigation between former employee and employer happens occasionally, but it's not common in Denmark.

Union umbrella agreements

An important part of flexicurity is unions, which are much less antagonistic towards management than they are in the US. Unions play a big role in corporate life, even for knowledge workers.

Some workplaces include employees from many different unions, often based on their area of education –

the engineers in one union, the communications team in another.

But certain industries, such as banking, have umbrella agreements with a single union. Everyone who works at a bank gets the benefits worked out by the Financial Services Employees Union Denmark.

The union as the touchpoint for complaints

When an employee has a complaint – whether it's harassment on the job, an unsafe working environment, or a payment dispute – the union is usually the first touchpoint, not the government or HR department.

At big companies, the union will have a *tillidsrepræsentant*, a sort of shop steward who is appointed from among the employees. That person will be the first contact for a staffer with a complaint.

At smaller firms, the employee may call the union directly and have the union call you.

Employee contract review

Unions are powerful, and union lawyers are up on all the latest developments in labor legislation.

They generally know enough not to get involved in a losing case, so if you hear from one of them concerning an employee, it's worth listening carefully.

In addition, some potential hires will ask for 48 hours

to run an employment contract past their union before accepting the job. This is standard, and not necessarily the sign of a troublemaker.

Finally, should you want to fire an employee, a union rep will help that employee negotiate the best possible termination agreement.

In fact, the shop steward is usually brought into the room as a witness if a union member is getting the chop.

Turn down the volume!

One of the great differences between Danes and Americans is their idea of what a good person is.

Americans think a good person is energetic, upbeat, friendly, confident, and able to fix things.

That's why Americans tend to bounce into a room with big smiles, big body language, and booming voices.

This can be a bit much for the Danes, who are by nature on a somewhat lower volume setting.

What is a good person?

For Danes, a good person is calm and reliable, doesn't stand out too much, and has a sharp sense of irony poised to take down anyone who thinks themselves high and mighty.

In a worst-case scenario, Americans can misinterpret this low-wattage approach as sourness and negativity – and to be fair, sometimes it is.

But more often, it's just a culture of self-restraint and a belief that a quality person, like a quality product, is self-evident.

Be yourself, but quieter

This is not to imply that Americans should hide who they are. Authenticity is important.

Just be aware that all that puppyish enthusiasm can be overwhelming to your Danish colleagues.

If you're accustomed to cranking the smile meter with a one-to-ten setting up to an 11, you may want to turn it down to a four to match your Danish team.

Selling to Danes

While Danes admire the dynamism and creativity of American business, they do not envy the American way of salesmanship.

The idea that somebody should pretend to be your very best friend until he succeeds in selling you something is upsetting to them.

Instead, Danes believe that a good product sells itself.

Don't exaggerate

Appealing to the emotional side of buying will be an immediate turnoff for your Danish contact.

So will exaggerating your product's benefits or overall success. Exaggeration is never appreciated in a Danish context; it corrodes trust.

Your Danish buyer is by nature skeptical. Deep product knowledge and a readiness to explain specific benefits will allow your product to "sell itself."

"Not invented here"

For a society that is generally open to the outside world, there's still a deep conviction that the Danish way is best.

You'll notice an enormous number of products with names beginning with "Dan" – from DanEgg in the supermarket to DanDryer for your hands in a public restroom.

Fruits and meats are often proudly identified as being of Danish origin, presumably because the farmers use fewer chemicals and take better care of their animals.

And someone with a degree from a Danish university will almost always be taken more seriously than someone with a non-Danish degree. (A Dane with an international degree on top of her Danish degree will be taken even more seriously.)

That means that as a non-Dane, you'll already be one step behind, and two steps behind if your product would benefit from a Danish-language interface and doesn't have one.

Extra research

As an outsider, it's particularly important to research how your product fits into the Danish market, whether or not there are any tax or regulatory angles in a Danish context, and how it will co-ordinate or compete with products already in use in the buyer's industry.

You will not be able to sell based on charm alone in Denmark.

The Danish calendar, and holiday weeks to avoid

Most online calendars contain a hidden setting for "week numbers," in which the first week of January is Week 1, running through Week 52 at the end of December.

These week numbers are widely used in Denmark. Your Danish colleagues may suggest a conference in Week 18 or inform you that they will be on vacation in Weeks 29, 30, and 31.

It's actually a clever system which gets rid of clumsy expressions like *How about the week beginning Monday, October 3?*

At any rate, you may want to activate the week number setting in your calendar so you know what your Danish colleagues are talking about.

Predictable vacation periods

Danes love their five weeks of vacation, but the good news is they tend to take them at predictable times, particularly if they have children in school.

The first big vacation week is Winter Holiday in mid-February (Week 7 or 8) when many families take off for a ski trip elsewhere in Europe. Denmark has few hills steep enough to ski down.

In spring comes Easter. The official public holidays stretch over five days, but many employees take extra days off before or afterwards, usually to open up the family's summer house.

Several one-day public holidays are sprinkled through the spring and are often used for teenagers' confirmations (a big deal in Denmark) or weddings.

Three-week summer holidays

Kids in Denmark get just six weeks off during the summer, from July to mid-August (Weeks 27 to 32). Their parents can be counted on to take at least three weeks off in a row during this period.

Fall holiday in October (Week 42) is a popular time for urban trips to Berlin, Budapest or New York. If you're visiting any major city during this period, you can expect to hear Danish spoken.

Finally, the Christmas season lasts from December 23 to January 2, with just a couple of poorly attended business days in the middle.

Plan your business around the holidays

Examine the Danish holiday calendar and confer with your Danish employees well in advance before planning a sales campaign or product launch.

Your team will not be open to re-arranging their vacations for you.

Asking anything more than a skeleton crew to work during these periods will be taken as the sign of a manager who "doesn't understand Denmark."

Good morning. Good day.

The English term *good morning* can be used anytime up until 11:59am, but in Denmark, *good morning* runs out around 10am, at which time it is succeeded by *good day* or a simple *hej*.

Saying *good morning* after 10am can sound sarcastic, as if you are implying that you're happy your colleague has finally turned up for work.

Watch out for "half seven"

Danes use military time – 16:00 instead of 4pm – when they want to be precise, but they may say *4 o'clock* in casual use.

Something to watch out for is that "half seven" in Danish corresponds to 6:30, while "half past seven" in English is 7:30.

Keep this in mind when making plans with Danish colleagues and clarify times if needed.

Managing Danes

Traditional top-down American bosses can struggle at first to lead their teams in Denmark, where the management culture is very different.

In a country where equality is king, merely thinking that you're in authority over someone else is a slightly comic position.

You may be the one who makes the final decision about products, staffing, and strategy, thinks the Danish employee, and *you might be the one who sits across from me at the annual employee evaluation*, but ***don't think you're better than me.***

Social welfare confidence

Part of this is the Danish social welfare system: "management by fear" is less effective when employees have access to two years of unemployment payments should they decide to leave their jobs. And their medical care and children's college prospects will be entirely unaffected.

But a bigger factor is the Danish child-raising and educational system. Children are raised to challenge their parents and their teachers, who they call by their first names.

In fact, the traditional Danish grading system (recently revised) used 11 for a flawless paper – but it was possible to achieve an even better grade, a 13, if your work was so spectacular that it taught the teacher something new.

Having an incentive to bust apart the status quo is the very basis of Danish innovation culture, and one of the reasons this tiny country punches above its weight on the world stage.

Everybody's opinion counts

What it means for you as a boss, however, is that nobody is going to carry out your orders just because you say so.

You need to earn respect, which isn't granted automatically.

Your team will expect to be consulted, expect to have their input collected, their questions answered, and their ideas acknowledged.

It's a much longer process, and if you see yourself as the kind of boss who likes to make snap decisions and turn on a dime, you may feel it limits you.

On the other hand, once you have worked hard to bring your team onside and earned their trust, they will follow you through fire.

Once they've committed to your project, it's their project too.

Keep calm in the workplace

Some American bosses have the unfortunate habit of shouting or losing their temper when things aren't going their way.

This baffles the peaceful Danes. Tantrums aren't a part of their culture, and they simply don't know how to react.

It's also hard for your Danish counterparts to judge how angry you really are. Does this outburst mean the relationship has been ruined forever? Or will they be expected to forget the whole thing once the problem has been resolved?

In a dramatic culture like the US, you may feel that a fiery outburst shows how much you care about the principle involved.

But to the Danes, you look immature and lacking in self-control.

Their weapon of choice is the sarcastic comment, or the passive-aggressive refusal to complete some task they secretly think is a waste of time.

"Jante Law" and why Danes underplay their skills

Many people believe equality is a desirable outcome. To make that happen, the short poppy must be helped to grow – and the tall poppy must be clipped off.

Tall poppy syndrome is what enforced equality is called in Australia, and in Denmark it's called the Law of Jante, after a novel from the 1930s.

Jante Law isn't a real law: it's a way of thinking in which it's considered good manners to underplay yourself, your skills, and your products.

At its best, this can result in delightful modesty and humility, an antidote to the constant self-promotion and pushiness that is part of American business life.

At its worst, Jante Law means petty envy and barely

concealed hatred directed towards people who are smarter or harder-working than you are.

It's no coincidence that most of the Danes I know who have chosen to move to the US have been energetic and innovative businesspeople, big personalities who didn't fit into little Denmark.

Danes undersell themselves

When doing business with Danes, be aware that they will probably be inclined to undersell themselves and their products.

It is anathema in Danish culture to promise something you cannot deliver, or to give your counterpart a "cat in a sack," an old farm expression for palming off a stray cat on someone who thought he was purchasing a tasty pig.

That means that Danes will under promise in order to make sure they are not overpromising.

You'll also notice this in Danish advertising, where no product is described as "better" or "the best."

This is because Danish marketing law only allows advertised products to be compared according to "specific, relevant, verifiable, and representative features," and *best* is rather subjective.

Generational change

There's a great deal of discussion in Denmark about

whether Jante Law is diminishing as new generations take their cues from the self-promotion common on social media.

While older Danes may have been brought up with the Jante Law basics – "Don't believe that you're anyone special" – younger people are more likely to be openly confident and careerist.

This is particularly true of people who work at the higher levels of US-affiliated companies.

Even so, an American-style elevator speech that makes you sound like a superhero will be poorly received by your Danish counterparts.

It's much better to speak calmly and humorously about your small successes and failures in business.

Admitting your imperfections makes you seem much more authentic – and much more likable – to the Danes.

Rating systems

A Dane recently told me about a misunderstanding he'd had with his American manager, who'd asked how things were going in his department.

"They're OK," the Dane said, meaning that the work was coming along in a satisfactory manner.

The US boss was concerned: he interpreted "OK" to mean that something was not satisfactory at all. If all were well, wouldn't his colleague have said, *"Great!"* or *"Super"* or even *"Excellent"*?

The American way of hyperbole meets its match in Danish understatement.

In Denmark, extreme understatement is a way of showing you're a good person with a sense of humor about yourself.

For example, a Danish man who has just won the Lotto and married the woman of his dreams might describe his mood as *slet ikke dårligt*, or "not bad at all."

Understatement vs hyperbole

If your company uses ratings systems for its products or managers, this culture of understatement may be reflected in the marks you get from Danish customers and colleagues.

A US customer might reflexively click on 10 when a company or product delivers everything it is supposed to deliver; anything less than 8 is a "bad score."

By contrast, a Dane might give 6 or 7 for the exact same performance.

They want to save the 10 for something really special.

Don't overdo it on the compliments

Americans love to give encouragement. They like to share the positivity. The US is, after all, the country that invented cheerleading.

But a boundless sea of compliments sounds artificial to the Danish ear.

From a Danish point of view, there are some things you are simply expected to do, such as the things you are hired for.

If you're doing them properly, no comment is required.

Constant applause

An American boss may feel she's being an inspirational leader by offering constant positive feedback – that she is bringing out the best in her people.

But her Danish team may feel they are being treated like children. *I am an adult professional. I don't need to constantly be applauded for doing my job.*

If you do give a compliment, it should be deeply felt, and you should be ready to elaborate on exactly what it is you found so impressive.

Cake to celebrate

That said, the Danes often say they envy the Americans' ability to celebrate success.

Success celebrations in Denmark are more modest. When things go well for your Danish team, it's traditional to bring a cake for everyone to share.

You don't have to bake the cake. Denmark has plenty of excellent bakeries, and to be honest most people would rather have a professionally made version.

Then choose a time in mid-afternoon, invite everyone involved, and perhaps make a two-minute speech re-iterating the highlights of the group's success.

And it is always a group success, even if everyone knows that one or two employees did most of the heavy lifting.

Celebrating bigger successes

For even bigger successes, such as an acquisition, companies sometimes throw a party with lots of food and lots of alcohol. (For Danes, it is not a party without a great deal of alcohol.)

If you plan to do this, announce it at least three months in advance.

Danes' calendars fill up quickly with family events and vacations, which is why Christmas parties should be announced in August at the latest.

Ambition and competitiveness

Most Danish schools do not give grades until children are 13 or 14, but there are occasional quizzes and such.

One day my daughter, who dislikes spelling, was pleased to find she'd done very well on a spelling quiz. She was eager to see how the other children had done and perhaps show off a little.

But when her teacher saw the kids discussing their marks, he quickly put a stop to it.

"Do not compare your score with the other children," he said. "Focus on your own work."

Do not compete against each other

If you've been brought up in an environment where competition is desirable and everyone knows who the top performers are, the Danish approach may be a bit of a shock.

Danish children – and adults – are not raised to compete against each other, and if you ask them to do so, they'll find it uncomfortable and distasteful.

This is a co-operative culture, where people generally work in groups and solidarity is seen as an important goal.

In a work environment, Danes will find it embarrassing if you single one employee out for doing well, or "hang out" an individual for doing poorly.

Competitive for products

That doesn't mean that Danes aren't competitive, but they are competitive for their product and service, not (at least openly) for themselves.

A survey[1] conducted of university students in 16 countries showed that only 49% of the young Danes surveyed hoped to go into management, compared to 77% of Americans surveyed.

Management responsibility in a corporate environment is seen as a headache by many Danes. Taxes will eat away much of the extra income, and a management job will require more hours at work, meaning less time with family.

On the other hand, entrepreneurship is popular.

---

1   *Building leaders for the next decade: How to support the workplace goals of Gen X, Gen Y, and Gen Z. Universum Generations Series, a collaboration with INSEAD Merging Markets Institute, the HEAD Foundation and MIT Leadership Center. 2017*

If I'm going to work crazy hours, think many Danes, *I'm going to start my own company*, either alone or with a group of like-minded colleagues. *Then the results of all that hard work flow back to me.*

Entrepreneurship and the "BMW Syndrome"

How big will those new startups grow? Some do very well, and some do just well enough to be sold to an enterprising buyer so the founder can go start a new company.

The "serial entrepreneur" is a staple of the Danish business media.

Other companies grow just big enough for the founder or founders to be satisfied with the income they have achieved and then plateau.

This is sometimes called the "BMW Syndrome." The point at which the founder can buy an expensive car (taxed at 150% of the purchase price) is the point at which the company tends to lose ambition.

Why do more when you've reached the limits of luxury in Denmark?

Gender equality in Denmark

Denmark has had two female prime ministers and about 40% of the people elected to the *Folketing*, their version of Congress, are women.

But when it comes to private industry, Danish women have one of the lowest participation rates in management in Europe. According to the OECD[1], about 26.5% of managers in Denmark are female, compared to 39.8% in the US.

It's not unusual to see a senior management team made up entirely of Danish males, with perhaps a Swedish or German male thrown in for diversity.

Most women work outside the home

That said, the majority of adult Danish women hold

---

1   *Organization for Economic Co-operation and Development 2018 statistics accessed from OECD.stat in June 2020.*

paying jobs. Stay-at-home parents are uncommon because the tax system makes it very difficult to survive on one income, even a hefty one.

For families with young children, the "Danish way" is for both parents to work full time and put the kids in government-run day care right after their first birthday.

Even the children of the Royal Family (including young Christian, the future King Christian XI of Denmark) did their time in government-run day care before moving into public schools.

Nannies are uncommon, although a few wealthy families have au pairs.

Danish men do housework

Danish men do more housework than any other men in the OECD nations, and are also deeply involved in childcare, although women still do more.

There's a certain expectation that even highly educated women with demanding jobs will bake buns (*boller*) from scratch, attend numerous parent meetings at the school or kindergarten, and plan cozy birthday parties for their children.

It's common for women with full-time jobs and young kids to be diagnosed with stress and take sick leave from work.

Time off vs career

Denmark's generous parental leave is supposed to be shared between parents but is, in practice, taken mostly by mothers. (That said, for creative-class men in Copenhagen and Aarhus, taking a few months of paternity leave has become a status symbol.)

I can say from personal experience that it's wonderful to have a paid year off to tend to and bond with a new baby.

A vast industry has sprung up to help new parents enjoy their child's first few months, offering baby swimming, baby music, baby yoga, and even baby psalm-singing at the local church.

Local governments even set up "mothers' groups" with five or six local mothers who have given birth at about the same time. They can share their various baby triumphs and troubles with other woman experiencing similar milestones.

Sometimes these groups click and the mothers and children become lifelong friends.

Interrupts the trajectory

But this paid time off does interrupt women's career trajectories, particularly because many Danish women choose to have two or three children in their 20s and 30s while their male counterparts are building business experience.

How much of the gender differences in management

is discrimination, and how much is personal choice? It's a difficult question to answer.

Some women try to split the difference and do part-time work while they raise their families, although in practice this can often morph into full-time work with part-time pay.

Don't expect chivalry

The blurring of traditional gender roles in Denmark has also eliminated traditional chivalry.

If you're a woman dating a Danish man, don't expect flowers, gifts, or to have him pick up the check for a romantic dinner.

In fact, if you're interested in a Danish man, it's always a good idea to take the initiative yourself.

Even in a non-dating environment, don't assume that a man will open doors for you or that a man will get up to let you have his seat on public transport when you have been standing (uncomfortably swaying) for a dozen stops.

A Danish man knows you can stand on your own two feet.

Differing concepts of privacy

A Danish friend was giving a speech to an industry organization in the US. As she introduced herself, she listed her professional accomplishments, then noted that she was 44 years old, divorced, and the mother of two wonderful children.

Some of the Americans in the audience were shocked. Why in the world would she reveal her age? And shouldn't her family status be her own personal business?

First of all, your age is rarely private in Denmark. Your birthdate, including the year, makes up the first six numbers of your CPR number, which is somewhat of a Social Security number on steroids that gives you access to everything from tax-funded medical care to library books.

It's very difficult to lie about your age to anyone who

has access to your CPR, right down to the guy who signs you up for your fitness center.

(The good news is that Danes tend to be more relaxed about signs of aging than Americans are. Photos of middle-aged celebrities, for example, often leave crow's feet and moles unretouched.)

Secondly, sharing family information in a business context is common in Denmark. Danes also frequently add it to their CV's to give a potential employer insight into themselves as a whole person.

Casual nudity

Casual nudity is also much more accepted in Denmark than it is in the US. Nude winter swimming in the chilly Danish harbors is a national passion, and even at the local swimming hall you'll be expected to get clean in the shared shower *without* your suit before diving in.

On the other hand, some things are more private in Denmark than they are in the US.

The standard mug shot you'll see in the US media whenever someone interesting has been arrested is unknown in Denmark.

Criminals are rarely pictured or named in the media, even after conviction. Images of a suspect on the loose are shared with the public only if the crime is very serious.

Why EU privacy laws are important

In addition, Denmark is part of the European Union's overall directive on privacy, which means you may have trouble accessing some websites from the US that don't comply with that directive.

The EU's privacy directive also includes the "right to be forgotten," which means that if you as an individual appear on someone's website and don't want to be there, you can approach them directly and ask for the item to be taken down.

I've done this myself a couple of times for old video interviews that were no longer relevant, and in both cases the item disappeared within an hour.

The downside is that other people can do this too, so if you find an important or delicate piece of information online that you'd like to refer to later, take a screen shot.

Privacy law affects marketing

EU privacy law will also affect your marketing efforts: there are very strict rules about what type of information you can send and who you can send it to.

Get used to seeing the initials "GDPR," which is what the General Data Protection Regulation is commonly called, and to hearing why it will prevent you from using that great direct marketing approach that worked so well in the US.

Danish meetings

Some Americans turn meetings into mini performances, in which they deliver a dazzling presentation that will enhance their position in the company and ultimately boost their careers.

Danes don't think of meetings the same way. Sure, they're interested in learning from a knowledgeable source, but they're expecting to be informed, not impressed.

Seeking consensus

Like many other aspects of Danish life, meetings are an equitable affair where everyone down to the student worker is expected to share information and then have his or her say, and in a best-case scenario consensus can be reached.

Sometimes this consensus-seeking goes on for far too long, resulting in a snap decision by the boss, who just can't take it any more.

No written agenda

Danish meetings don't always have a written agenda, but they usually have a declared purpose, and it's a good idea to be prepared before you go in.

The quickest way to lose a Dane's respect is to waste their time.

Sadly, some Danish meetings will waste your time, as they meander about and wander off into side alleys.

Assuming that the meeting has a set endpoint, it's OK to get up at that time and claim another engagement.

Meeting refreshments

It's common to have a bowl of sweets at a Danish meeting; despite their glowing good health, Danes are among the world's top consumers of candy.

When external customers are present, this is sometimes upgraded to cake or a fruit plate.

Everyone pours their own coffee in a Danish meeting, and usually tidies up their own dishes afterwards.

Language concerns

As a non-Danish speaker, your presence will mean the meeting must be held in English.

This is usually not a problem for younger members of the team, but some older staff may feel a little shy in English.

Often these older employees have important product or customer knowledge. Yet they may be reluctant to make points and pose questions in front of the group because they're not confident of their language abilities.

You can counteract this by asking specifically for their opinion, or by taking them aside later one-to-one and asking if they have any concerns.

When to schedule a meeting

In Danish families with young children, one parent generally drops off the kids at school or the local day care center, while the other picks up the kids at the end of the day.

If you are so foolish as to schedule a meeting before 9am or after 3pm, you risk upsetting this family system.

The parents will have to switch places, or one parent will have to do both drop-off and pick-up, and everyone will be in a sour mood.

Avoid headaches by scheduling your meetings between 9:30am and 2:30pm.

If you insist on planning a meeting outside those hours, people will be there if they have to be, but they won't be happy about it.

Don't say "Let's have lunch" unless you mean it

Maybe you're just being your usual outgoing self, chatting with a Danish contact or business partner, and a big event in your life comes up in conversation.

You could be going through a divorce or a complex fertility process, or perhaps a family member has been involved in a crime and is struggling with the court system.

Whatever it is, it's close to your heart and you can't help talking about it, sometimes in depth, in that open-hearted way familiar to viewers of afternoon talk shows.

Danes usually don't talk about such intimate things with people they don't know well. So when you do, they immediately think *Now we are friends*.

Friendship is a deep relationship

For Danes, friendship is a deep and often lifelong relationship. It means you can rely on each other through thick and thin.

From your point of view, you were just getting something off your chest, but from their point of view, sharing such intimate experiences is a form of commitment.

When it doesn't turn out that way, there are hurt feelings and sometimes a bit of anger that Americans are so flaky and superficial.

Danes don't understand fuzzy promises

This is also true of more casual statements. "Let's have lunch sometime," you may say to someone just to get them off the phone or put an end to an overlong chat.

It never occurs to your Danish contact that you have only a flimsy intent of actually having lunch with him.

The same is true for other statements of intent, like "Let's get together for a beer" or "We should definitely go for a run around the lakes at some point."

Danes are quite literal-minded and don't understand the fuzzy nature of these promises. They will be looking forward to the beer or the run around the lakes and rather hurt when it never comes to pass.

Alternately, they may say quite bluntly, "Thanks, but I

really don't have time to go for a run with you."

That may sound rude to you, but to your Danish contact, honesty and directness are better than airy promises that will never be fulfilled.

What Danes think of Americans

Generally Danes like Americans, and Americans like to be liked, which is a good basis for business and business relationships. Danes see Americans as friendly, open, and positive.

That said, the Danish media feeds its readers a steady diet of all the most shocking things that 350 million Americans can come up with, with a special emphasis on anything that feeds pre-existing prejudices about obesity, guns, and social discord.

The "Bible Belt" appears frequently in Danish media as the sort of thing its readers should look down upon.

Big brother must be cut down to size

Denmark is a small country, so it's not always evident to your Danish business contact that something going on in rural Oregon doesn't entirely reflect your experiences in suburban Wisconsin or vice-versa.

And when Danes talk about the US, the Danish anti-authoritarian streak is often visible. "Big Brother" countries must be constantly cut down to size.

Danes have a similar relationship to Sweden, and the Danish media take a peculiar glee in reporting anything going wrong there.

American culture is popular

Danes do like American culture, in particular American music.

In Jylland, the part of Denmark with the most farms and agriculture, US country music is popular. There are even square-dancing clubs.

US gospel music is popular all over Denmark; several small cities have their own gospel choirs. It's inspiring to see large groups of Danes embracing music that is part of the cultural heritage of Black America.

Many Danes also like to follow American sports, particularly basketball and NFL football.

Baseball, on the other hand, looks a lot like the Danish children's game of roundball, and to see big strong men playing it for money looks to them like a professional league for Duck Duck Goose.

Thoughts on American food

American food consumption habits are likely to come up in conversation. McDonald's is big in Denmark, and some Danes seem convinced that Americans eat nothing else.

If you're welcoming Danish business contacts to the US, try introducing them to Kansas City BBQ, New England crab cakes, California Asian fusion cuisine, New Orleans gumbo, or some excellent TexMex.

There are a few TexMex restaurants in Denmark, but quality is often lacking. I never had a brown Margarita until one was served to me in Denmark.

When Denmark is in the media

Being citizens of a petite country that plays a minor role on the world stage, Danes are thrilled whenever they are mentioned in the international media.

Their European football championship in 1992 is something they love to discuss – they beat Germany, another big brother country! – and so is a visit by Oprah to Denmark in 2009. (She stopped by one of the most expensive apartments in Copenhagen and marveled at the huge windows and fabulous view from this "typical Danish home.")

If a story about Denmark appears on any major US website or TV channel while you are doing business with the Danes, they may ask if you have seen it and then launch into an explanation of how the American reporter got it wrong.

Know your famous Danes

It's also not a bad idea to do a Google search for "World's Most Famous Danes" before you head out for a social occasion with your Danish colleagues.

They are very proud of the athletes, actors, and musicians on this ever-changing list, and they will be impressed and somewhat touched that you know who they are.

Small talk with Danes

Americans sometimes find silence uncomfortable. When conversation flags, they often try to fill up the empty space with random chatter, stilted laughter, or in a worst-case scenario, whistling and humming.

Danes, like most Northern Europeans, don't feel this way. They are comfortable with silence.

What they find stressful is small talk.

Automating it away

Having to make small talk is so intimidating that one of my customers, an engineering firm, asked if they might be able to automate it in their emails to their American colleagues.

They suggested a program that would scrape their colleagues' local weather report – "I hear you're having a lot of rain over there!" and sports reports, "Tough loss in the fourth quarter!" – and automatically insert them into the opening lines of the email, leaving the engineers to focus on actual business.

Don't say "How are you?"

In particular, Danes hate the question *How are you?*

They don't know how to answer it, and sometimes get frustrated with their American colleague who asks the question and then doesn't have the patience to listen to an in-depth answer.

I recommend avoiding *How are you?* entirely.

Either pare it down to a slim *Good to see you!* or flip it to a quick yes-or-no question like "Did you get out and enjoy the good weather this weekend?" Alternately, prepare a more detailed question related to the person's business role.

Small talk with Danes

If you're invited to a Danish dinner party or company holiday party, you'll find yourself in a situation where you need to make small talk with Danes for hours.

Most dinner parties are set up at long tables where you'll be fixed in place, leaving you with the option of talking to the person on your right, the person on your left, and occasionally the people across the table from you, depending on the noise level.

Reliable topics include travel (the Danes love to go places during their annual five weeks of vacation), gardening and home renovation, amateur sports clubs they may be involved with, and all of the ways Denmark is better than the United States – a topic the Danes never tire of.

If you enjoy talking US politics, the Danes will too, although you'll enjoy this more if you are a Democrat than if you are a Republican.

Topics to steer clear of

Topics to steer clear of include personal finance and salaries, the Danish Royal Family (many people adore them, others call them "Denmark's biggest welfare recipients"), and anything that would make you appear to be bragging about your own family's accomplishments.

There's also no need to expound on whether or not you have Danish ancestry if it goes any further back than your own parents.

The Danes will politely nod at your connections to the Danish ethnic family, but they will find it about as interesting as you would find the discovery of a previously unknown second cousin once removed.

Danish patriotism

I once heard a man say that no country in the world displayed its flag as much as the Americans did.

That man had clearly not been to Denmark, where the Danish flag appears on cakes, Christmas trees, and even plastic cucumber wrapping.

The Danes love their flag, which is the oldest in the world in continuous use and the model for similar flags used by Sweden, Norway, Finland, and Iceland.

Danish flags and birthdays

In particular, the Danish flag is associated with birthdays. Should your birthday come around while you are in Denmark, your colleagues may put a cloth Danish flag on a little brass flagpole in your workspace or by your plate at lunch.

This isn't a political symbol. It just means "joy."

When members of the Danish Royal Family have birthdays, tiny cloth flags are attached to many of the local buses.

It's a national sport to figure out who is being celebrated, often someone who is entirely forgotten for the rest of the year.

Danes love their Constitution

The Danes are as fond of their Constitution as the Americans are, and it is frequently cited whenever a legal dispute is in the news.

Constitution Day is celebrated with a half-day off every June 5, and people accused of a crime in Denmark are taken to court for a "constitutional hearing."

When I became a Danish citizen, I was sent in the mail a small paperback version of the Danish constitution.

While admirable, it is also complex and wordy, lacking the simple poetry of the US Bill of Rights. I must admit I never read it all the way through.

The Danish military

The Danish military is small – only about 12,000 active-duty personnel – and co-operates extensively with the US military. Danish Air Force pilots are trained in Texas, for example.

Denmark still has a military draft. Every man turning 18 gets a number that may or may not be called up, and there are usually not enough spots for everyone who would like to serve.

Being a soldier or a sailor in Denmark doesn't generate the automatic respect sometimes given to members of the US military.

That said, the Royal Life Guards, which guard the Royal Family, are an extremely high-status group.

In addition to general army training, the Life Guards stand long hours wearing tall bearskin hats outside the various palaces, protecting the royalty inside.

The Life Guards are where the future titans of Denmark meet each other, and saying their child is a member of *Livgarden* is one of the few things Danish parents dare to brag about.

Design in Denmark

Design is a passion in Denmark, particularly interior design, which makes perfect sense in a culture where people spend so much time in their homes during the long, dark winter.

Danish design furniture, with its simple, elegant lines, is popular (and widely counterfeited) all over the world.

Utility and grace in every setting

Even outside the home, you'll notice that things in Denmark are carefully set up to flow with maximum utility and grace, from the beautiful new circular line of the Copenhagen metro to the sleek new bicycle bridge across Odense Harbor, to the circular rainbow walk atop the Aarhus art museum to the curvy, streamlined toilets found in every public restroom.

I even notice the difference when I fill out my tax forms, which I have the privilege of doing for both the Danish tax authorities and the IRS.

The American forms look like they were designed by a yawning bureaucrat using fifteen-year-old software.

The Danish tax forms are clear, concise, and gorgeous – although the tax rates are also much more ambitious.

Make design a priority

What this means in business terms is that whatever you produce or deliver in Denmark, whether it is a product or promotional materials, must be beautifully designed, preferably by a Dane.

American style can look boxy and obvious to Danish eyes.

Don't ever give your Danish business partners something put together by an amateur, or anything printed on shoddy paper or made with cheap materials.

In the Danish market a low price is welcome, but quality and polish are much more important.

Working for a Danish boss

Interviewing for a job in Denmark and working with a Danish team are topics I've covered in more detail in my previous book, *How to Work in Denmark.*

Here, however, are a few general rules about working for a Danish boss.

Independence vs inspiration

Being a boss is a funny kind of position in Denmark, a thoroughly anti-authoritarian culture.

Bosses are breaking one of the first rules of Denmark by being, in fact, in authority over others, so they tend to compensate by not being too domineering.

This means Danish bosses provide much more independence and much less guidance and inspiration than you are accustomed to in the US.

Ask your Danish boss how you should tackle a problem and she may say, "*Well, how do you think you should handle it?*"

Fewer specific instructions

Expect much less in the way of specific instructions and much more discussion of process and how to reach a consensus.

Indirect orders are common. "I think it would be useful to have this done by Friday," means, in fact, that it should be done by Friday. Ask if you're not sure.

Bosses in Denmark also don't need to pretend they're all-seeing or all-knowing, as US bosses sometimes do.

"I'm not sure – ask someone on my team," is a perfectly reasonable thing for a Danish boss to say.

More trust, less monitoring

You will not be monitored as much in Denmark and you will be trusted more, but that trust is something that you must treat as precious.

Calling in sick when you're not really sick is not done in Denmark. Take a "personal day" instead.

And never say you understand a concept when you really don't quite get it, or insist you've got a situation under control when you really haven't.

These are behaviors that will destroy a Danish boss's trust in you.

Boss for now, not forever

Jobs in Denmark are almost never lifetime appointments, so one of the most important things you can get from your employer is continuing education in your field.

At the annual "employee conversation," make sure to come equipped with a few suggestions for courses or conferences that will serve both the company's interests and your own.

These events will make sure that your knowledge is up-to-date and help you fill up your LinkedIn connections (Danes love LinkedIn) with the sort of contacts in your industry that will help you get your next job with your next Danish boss.

The visitor who wasn't equal

An American businesswoman made a big mistake while visiting her company's Danish office.

She flew into the local airport, rented a car, drove to the office, and met with the top person there.

Then she got back in the car, drove back to the airport, and flew away.

Meeting just with the top person – and not taking the time to greet the rest of the people in the office – was a crime against equality.

Shake everyone's hand

The correct thing to do would have been to schedule enough time in Denmark to go through the office and meet every person on the team, at the very least for a quick handshake and a few moments of business-related conversation.

Even better would have been scheduling enough time to join the group lunch that is common in Danish offices.

Even better than that would have been a few "get to know you" meetings with the various teams and team leaders to show that she was interested in their projects and was aware of their concerns.

Don't drop by

In fact, the only thing the visitor did right was to schedule her visit well in advance and send a detailed agenda so that the person she was meeting could be fully prepared.

Danes are not spontaneous people, in either their professional or social lives. It is common for them to make plans months ahead.

Never "drop in" on a Dane unexpectedly. On the other hand, if you accept an invitation, don't cancel unless you are ill.

If a Dane has put aside time for you, he has offered you a bit of his most valuable resource.

Assume everyone is useful

There is little dead wood in Danish companies. People are simply too expensive, and the termination process too straightforward, particularly if layoffs are done in groups or buyouts are offered.

Reliably assume that everyone you meet has a useful role, regardless of their title, since Danes generally don't care that much about titles anyway.

This includes student workers, usually college or graduate students who are invited to meetings. The company hopes to hire the best ones for full-time jobs as soon as they are available.

Be kind to the piccoline

In fact, the only people not included in meetings are the office handyman and the *piccolo* or *piccoline*, usually a very young person hired to clean up the kitchen and occasionally act as receptionist.

That said, these people should also be treated with respect and never with irritation, no matter how busy or frustrated you might be with your schedule or travel arrangements or your inability to type in the wireless password.

If you snap at somebody in a Danish office, everyone will hear about it, and your reputation will not be enhanced.

Negotiating with Danes

Danes have a great love of transparency – which they see as an element of one of their other great loves, authenticity – and this is reflected in their negotiation style.

They're not there to play 4D chess or create drama at peak moments.

They're there to get a deal done that can potentially build a long-term relationship based on openness and trust.

Extreme transparency

Sometimes the Danes can be so transparent that it seems a little comic.

An acquaintance told me how she was chatting with a Danish business associate before an upcoming negotiation.

"What's your top bid?" she asked him.

"Fifty," said her associate.

"What's your opening bid?"

"Fifty," he replied.

Co-operation in a small country

That doesn't mean the Danes are suckers. With centuries of merchant tradition behind them, they enjoy a good business deal.

In particular, people from Jylland are known for being tough negotiators.

But like so many things in Denmark, the negotiation approach is based on co-operation instead of confrontation.

It's important to remember that Denmark is a small country and everyone knows everyone, specifically within industries.

If you're found to be a cheat, overly dramatic, or an unreliable partner, word will get around quickly.

Simple, practical agreements

Denmark is a much less litigious society than the US, so your Danish partner will assume a handshake deal is valid long before the written contracts arrive.

Alternately, your partner will outline the points of your agreement in an email and ask you to reply "OK" if you agree. This serves as a quick 'n' dirty written contract.

It's important to know, however, the Danes have an extremely flexible and practical approach to business.

When market conditions change, they will often try to adjust agreements to match.

The Danish way of customer service

In a large, highly competitive market like the US, you often do cartwheels to keep your customer happy.

This is less true in Denmark, a small market that is somewhat protected by the limited number of people who speak Danish.

In Denmark, the needs of a company's employees are often considered equal to if not more important than the needs of its customers.

For example, on Christmas Eve, the buses in many Danish cities stop running from 5pm until 11pm so the bus drivers can eat Christmas Eve dinner with their families.

Bus riders who want to eat dinner with *their* families should plan to arrive by 4pm and stay until midnight.

No "go above and beyond"

Danish customers haven't been conditioned to expect all the go-above-and-beyond and extra freebies that American customers often demand.

A bad night in a hotel with the fire alarm going off by accident twice won't get you a free stay; a request for water while dining in a restaurant will result in the server opening an expensive bottle.

An acquaintance leased an expensive luxury car and, as he was leaving the showroom, asked for a plastic phone holder for the dashboard. He was charged $15 for it.

Internationals living in Denmark constantly complain about bad customer service and, if they are nonwhite, sometimes see it as racially motivated. Racism does exist in Denmark, but lousy customer service is widely available to all.

Danes repatriating from the US usually say that American customer service is what they miss most.

A good product sells itself

In Danish shops, salespeople are sometimes lackadaisical or invisible.

A business contact of mine opened a little shop selling high-end Danish souvenirs – Danish whisky, Danish honey, Danish art posters – but after a trial period, stopped hiring Danish personnel in favor of internationals only.

She said her inventory required storytelling and introduction – *"This honey was collected from a hive on top of Copenhagen City Hall"* – and the Danish hires didn't feel comfortable doing that.

Shouldn't a good product sell itself? they thought, while hanging out around the cash register.

Nobody wanted to be pushy.

Crime and punishment

Denmark is a low-crime society, but it is not a no-crime society.

Your smartphone or laptop will disappear quickly if left in the wrong place, bicycle theft is common, and the country has the unhappy position of being Europe's number-one spot for home burglaries. Thieves just can't resist those great Danish design housewares.

That said, penalties are not as draconian as they sometimes are in the US. Many prisons work on the "open plan" where convicted individuals can come and go to work, school and other approved activities while serving their sentence.

Since everyone in Denmark has to register their home

address with the state and use a government-provided number for the health and banking systems, it's hard to run away and hide for very long.

A big, fat fine

Instead of prison, what the Danes really love is a fine – a big, fat fine.

Caught speeding in your car? That will be $600. Bicyclists can be fined too: $100 for riding on the sidewalk, $200 for running a red light, or $300 for biking while intoxicated.

Fines are also imposed if you ride the bus, metro, or train without precisely the right ticket.

The roving "controllers" are merciless professionals who won't buy your claim of being a confused foreigner and will sometimes take you off the train to discuss payment.

Most Danes have stories about getting caught by the controllers themselves.

Pay your taxes

The crime that you really must be sure not to commit, however, is tax evasion.

The Danish social welfare system relies on everyone paying their share, and people or companies who are revealed to be cheaters will find their reputations in tatters.

Fortunately, the Danish tax department is somewhat

more accessible and interactive than the IRS.

You or your accountant can call and chat about precisely how big your tax should be.

Danish humor and conflict avoidance

Humor and aggression are mixed up with each other in Denmark, a conflict-adverse society that can use a joke either to lighten the mood or deliver a withering put-down – and it can be hard to tell which is which.

Danes use sarcasm so frequently that they sometimes forget they're doing it.

And they rarely smile at their own joke, or add a disclaimer like "Just kidding." Instead, the statement simply hangs in the air.

Was it funny? Was it nasty? Was it both?

Combined with some Americans' eagerness to be offended, this toxic brew can eat away at cross-cultural teamwork.

Equality and Danish humor

Danish humor has its roots in the country's passion for equality: everyone, no matter how high or how low, is expected to be able to make fun of themselves.

Being able to take a joke – to not take yourself too seriously – is an important part of being considered a good person in Denmark.

And unlike Americans, who make fun of situations, Danes go directly to making fun of *people*.

If you mention, for example, that the breakfast in your hotel was sub-par, some witty colleague might say, "Well, you're American. You ought to be used to bad food."

The joy of human imperfectability

Cutting remarks can also be used to discipline people who step out of line, or to cut someone down to size if they break the diktats of equality.

But Danish humor can also joyfully celebrate human imperfectability, as it does with the "failure beer" (*kvajebajer*) or, during working hours, the "failure cake."

When you've made an avoidable mistake, the Danish way is to admit it and buy a beer for everyone who has seen you fumble, or offer the team an afternoon cake. Cake brings people together in Denmark.

For Americans, admitting you were wrong can be

difficult, in part because you don't want to lose your air of authority, and in part because you don't want to get sued.

It's more tempting to try to cover your backside or blame someone else.

But owning up to your fumbles and missteps can go a long way towards earning you the respect of your Danish team.

Denmark is not just Copenhagen

One of the things that surprised me when I first moved to Denmark is that there could be so many distinctions and divisions between fewer than six million people living in an area half the size of Indiana.

But the differences exist, and they are deeply felt.

Stopping by Copenhagen and saying you've seen Denmark is a little bit like stopping by Manhattan and Disney World and saying you've seen the United States. (And many Danes do precisely this.)

Dry humor in Jylland

While Copenhagen is both the capital of the country and its business center, much of the country's wealth is generated in Jylland, the large land mass stuck to Germany.

Jylland is the source of most of Denmark's agricultural exports, particularly pork, and many of its best engineers, who these days largely concern themselves with green energy technology.

People from Jylland are known for their extremely dry humor and low excitement levels, which become more pronounced the further north you go.

I found this out for myself when I brought my "How to Live in Denmark Game Show" comedy presentation to Brande, a town of about 7000 out in the countryside. The same jokes that had wowed audiences numerous times elsewhere in the country earned only stone-faced silence, and the occasional upturned mouth corner.

After it was over, I apologized to the organizer, and said I was sorry that they hadn't liked the show.

"What do you mean?" she said. "They had a great time."

"This is how they look when they're having a great time."

Different regional accents

Danes from various parts of Denmark also have sharply different accents. Some regional dialects, like *Bornholmsk* and *Sønderjysk*, are so specialized that people speaking them are subtitled on Danish TV.

It's common for urban types to make fun of people who speak like they come from the countryside, calling them *bonderøv*, or "farmer butts."

The "proper" dialect-free version of Danish is *rigsdansk* – Danish as spoken by the monarch. In addition, there is a government agency that updates the dictionary, approves spellings, and produces complex rules about commas that have even highly educated Danes tearing their hair out.

On a daily basis, most Danes speak a casual, urban form of the language, peppered with English words and a good deal of English-language profanity.

Many think these words are fun and colorful and have no idea why anyone might be offended by them.

Drive the Daisy Route

If you have a good amount of time in Denmark and are itching to get behind the wheel of a car, consider taking a short trip along *The Marguerite Route*, otherwise known as the Daisy Route, a 2200-mile network of small roads through the prettiest parts of the Danish countryside.

You'll see the magnificent white-sand beaches of West Jylland, the straw-roofed houses in villages on Fyn, the treacherous chalk cliffs at Møns, and the beautiful castle at Helsingør that features in Shakespeare's "Hamlet."

Taking a weekend off to explore the Danish countryside will give you a sense of the natural diversity of this green, peaceful country, something you can't fully appreciate in the taxi between your office and the airport.

Driving in Denmark

While a car is useful for exploring the Danish countryside, a car in one of Denmark's larger cities can be a millstone around your neck.

The traffic is terrible, the fuel costs stratospheric, the parking spaces doll-sized. Bicyclists own the road and often ignore traffic rules.

Even if the company you're visiting is in the suburbs or exurbs, there's a good chance you'll save money by taking a cab – and most Danish taxis are Mercedes-Benz or Teslas. (There is no Uber or Lyft in Denmark.)

Watch out for bicyclists

If you do choose to drive in the city, be very careful about right turns. Several Danish bicyclists are killed every year because a car or truck took a right turn and the bicyclist (who may be drunk, on his phone, or simply not paying attention) continued going straight.

There is no legal right turn on red in Denmark, and even on green, the bicyclist has the right of way.

You might choose to bike to work yourself, which is common in Denmark, even for executives. Many offices contain showers so commuters can clean up and change into their business gear.

If you do bike, don't dawdle in the bike lanes – these people are commuters, this is rush hour, and they don't want a gawking tourist clogging up their passing lane.

150% tax on new cars

Denmark has never had a car industry, which is why the government is able to get away with such high car taxes – 85% to 150% of the purchase price of a new vehicle – and why many Danish cities actively discourage car traffic.

Most Danes are good drivers, although they have a weird fondness for U-turns at unexpected moments.

While the Danes are hearty drinkers, the penalties for driving while intoxicated are substantial.

A blood alcohol level above 0.5% will get you in trouble, so if you've had more than a single glass of wine or beer, call a cab.

Dining with the Danes

Unlike the Norwegians, Swedes, and some Germans, the Danes don't show their cultural pride by dressing up in 19th century folklore outfits. (The first time I ever saw a Danish version was at a Danish culture festival in Solvang, California.)

Instead, Danes express their cultural pride through food.

When visiting Denmark, you'll be offered Danish cuisine, and expressing enthusiasm for it will go a long way towards generating harmony with your Danish colleagues.

Vegans and carnivores

Danish cuisine has something for everyone. If you're a carnivore, don't miss the Danish pork dishes, particularly *flæskesteg*, the crispy, fatty fried pork that's the official national food.

For people who prefer fish, there's a great selection in this country surrounded by water. Curried herring and fried plaice are popular, and so are many types of salmon. I like the thinly-sliced smoked salmon served on rye bread with chives, dill, and a bit of chopped red onion.

Vegans can enjoy a great selection of root vegetables, wonderful fresh Danish berries, or the sweet elderflower juice that is sometimes blended with vodka or champagne.

Denmark's famous thick bread, *rugbrød*, is vegan-friendly and can be eaten with potatoes on top as a type of *smørrebrød*, the open-faced sandwiches that are popular at lunchtime.

Sweet tastes

Danes adore cake and candy, in particular salt licorice, which is a national passion.

Make room in your food plan for a real Danish pastry, which are nothing like the ones you get in a plastic bag from the vending machine at home. Made daily with fresh cream and the famous Danish butter, they are worth every calorie.

There's also an old-fashioned dessert called *rødgrød med fløde*, a kind of berry porridge. I've never been served this dish in real life, but Danes think it's hilarious to try to make foreigners pronounce it.

At a restaurant

Much of your dining with the Danes will probably be lunches at corporate canteens, which all but the very smallest employers provide for their employees.

"Going out for lunch" is rare in Denmark, and some smaller towns may not even have restaurants open at this time of day.

A weekday breakfast at a restaurant is very unusual, although weekend brunch is popular in the big cities.

At any time of day, your restaurant experience will be different in Denmark than in the US, because Denmark has no cheap labor or tipping culture.

Employees are highly paid and there are fewer of them. In many cafés, you'll order at the bar, pay in advance, and then pick up your own food when it's ready.

If you do have a server, they will not be particularly attentive – no refills! – and the chef won't be accustomed to making changes to the menu based on your allergies or dietary preferences.

Most restaurant kitchens close at 9pm, and unless the place is also a bar, you're expected to be out the door by 10pm.

Tipping is not required, although you can always slightly "round up," paying DK200 for a DK185 bill, for example.

Don't rush home

In the US, dining out is often part of a longer evening. You go to dinner and a movie, or dinner and out for drinks and dancing afterwards.

In Denmark, the dinner is the evening.

Whether dining at a business contact's home or in a restaurant, you are expected to sit in one chair for many hours, conversing with the people on both sides of you and polishing off multiple bottles of wine or beer.

When I first arrived in Denmark, I unintentionally offended many people by leaving too early.

I was thinking from the American point of view: I didn't want to stay too long and make myself a nuisance.

That's not how the Danes think. Long evenings are something you will have to get used to, along with some Danes' disconcerting habit of eating a hamburger with a knife and fork.

Avoid cheerful hot air

Americans love inspirational items.

Whether it's a poster that says "Today is a good day to realize how far you've come" or a notepad that says "Storms don't last forever" or even a book called "100 Pep Talks" (all of which I recently found in a single store in Atlanta's Ponce City Market), there's always a market for slogans that provide encouragement for life in a competitive society.

Danes don't do this kind of optimistic self-help. They are ruthlessly practical people who think in precise, factual terms.

We're number one!

Some American bosses like to energize their teams with chanting similar to a political or sports rally: *"We're number one!" "We can do it!" "We will win!"* or other uplifting slogans.

This will have your Danish employees rolling their eyes.

According to which parameters are we number one? they might ask. *And why is being number one useful when it comes to achieving our corporate mission and vision, serving our customers, and creating a better workplace?*

If you try to pump up your team with cheerful hot air, they will think you are silly.

Mindfulness yes, astrology no

In general, appeals to the inspirational or spiritual side of life fall flat for the Danes, who are nominally Christian but in practice go to church only for baptisms, confirmations, weddings, and funerals.

While mindfulness and meditation are popular as stress relievers, new-age religions like astrology, crystals, and psychics are seen as odd or immature.

Don't ask your new Danish colleague what his sun sign is and then predict you'll work together harmoniously.

The only exception is numerology, perhaps because Danes are so deeply proud of their names.

I know of more than one Danish woman who has changed her name in mid-life in order to change her luck, based on what her numerologist recommended.

Health care and the Danish social welfare system

When visiting the US recently, I stopped in a diner for breakfast and ordered eggs and toast.

"What type of bread would you like for your toast?" the server asked. "We have white, wheat, rye, sourdough, pumpernickel, cinnamon raisin, and bagels."

The overwhelming toast selection is a rough metaphor for the US health system: so many options it can be overwhelming, along with labyrinthine insurance systems and ludicrous billing.

There are no diners in Denmark, but if you go to a restaurant, they will offer you one type of bread.

Tax-funded, with fewer choices

This corresponds to the Danish public health system. It

is tax-funded and you will rarely have to fill out a form, but you will have fewer choices.

The state will tell you what you are eligible for and when you are eligible to receive it. Urgent care is delivered efficiently, but for non-urgent care you may have to wait a bit.

This is why millions of Danes pay for additional private insurance, and it is a staple of corporate recruitment packages.

And while *over treatment* is a problem in the US – along with "defensive medicine" and too many tests – *under treatment* is common in Denmark.

Don't be surprised if you're told to take the equivalent of a Tylenol and a nap for everything from knee pain to recovery from a C-section.

Social welfare is popular

Danes love their cradle-to-grave welfare state. In two decades of living here, I've never met a single person who wanted it dismantled.

But it is a commitment, a national commitment. Everyone with the ability to work *must* work, and must pay substantial taxes, in order to finance the services shared by all.

At the same time, everyone accepts that there will be

limits on services so there are enough to go around.

For example, many expensive new drugs are simply not offered in Denmark, even if they could save the lives of individual patients.

There's only so much money that can be spent on health, and in the Danish system, it must be distributed as equally as possible.

What it means to you

The Danes use the word "welfare" to cover not just direct income transfers, but universal health, unemployment compensation, and tax-financed education.

To keep everyone honest, the system is sometimes an iron fist in a velvet glove.

So while unemployment payments are generous – up to 90% of your working income for as long as two years – receiving them requires regular visits with a personal job counselor and proof that you are actively looking for work.

This may drive you crazy if you are a hiring manager, since you will receive half-hearted applications from people who are sending them only to satisfy their job counselor.

Homelessness and basic income

Even if they can't (or won't) find work, very few people are down and out in Denmark: homelessness is much less common than it is in the USA.

Danes who have exhausted every other resource can get a small basic income, although they are required to sell non-essential assets like jewelry and motorcycles before they are eligible.

Only legal residents of Denmark can receive this assistance, and many Danish homeless shelters accept legal residents only. If you see someone sleeping rough, they are likely to be a migrant.

Begging is illegal in Denmark – police do make arrests – and unauthorized encampments in urban areas are illegal too. Danish police quickly clear these camps away.

You'll often see migrants collecting cans and bottles in order to redeem the deposit at local supermarkets.

If you're drinking beer in a park (which is allowed in Denmark) collectors may ask if you're finished with your bottle so they can take it and exchange it for cash.

Some things you don't get

Many Americans who are fans of the Danish social welfare system assume if offers everything they get in the US, plus more.

They usually miss the half of the equation in which they will also have to *give* much more in taxes, plus accept limits on what they receive.

For example, Danish universities are tax-funded, so

students pay no tuition and even receive a small stipend to live on while they study.

But there are limited spaces in many of the popular subjects, such as journalism and dentistry.

If you don't get one of those slots, you'll have to rethink your life choices, or study abroad and miss building up the local network that is so important to career success.

The "happiest country in the world"

When I hear that Denmark is the "happiest country in the world," I'm skeptical, but I do believe Danes have fewer daily worries because of their social welfare system.

Plenty of individuals manage to manufacture their own unhappiness by cheating on their partners, drinking too much alcohol, living beyond their means, and other classic vices.

When there are no foreigners around, Danes have plenty of complaints (or *brok*, which rhymes with "clock") about the lapses and blunders of their social welfare system.

(One classic joke: "*We don't have capital punishment in Denmark. Instead, we have the public health service.*")

But to the outside world, they will defend it as passionately as they defend the Danish flag.

Diversity and the Danes

In southern Florida, "Manatee mailboxes" are popular. To show your support for conserving local wildlife, you can order a five-foot-tall fiberglass version of this dolphin-like animal to cradle your mailbox in its fins.

It's crazy and fun and a little bit weird – and it's utterly unthinkable in Denmark, where practicality and modesty are the order of the day.

Being different just for the sheer whimsy of it is not the Danish way.

One American mother told me of collecting her daughter from the government day care center only to find that all her colorful hair ribbons had been taken out.

"It made her look too different from the other children," the day care worker said.

Danish with an accent

Although Copenhagen, Aarhus, Esbjerg, and Odense have been trading cities for centuries and are accustomed to a wide range of humans, much of Denmark is still a series of villages where people have lived for centuries.

Outsiders are always a little suspect. Even Danes who move from one part of Denmark to another say it can be almost impossible to make friends.

And while you're probably accustomed to hearing English spoken in many different ways, Danes are not used to hearing Danish spoken with a foreign accent.

Almost every international who has taken pains to learn Danish has a story about their pronunciation being mocked and laughed at, along with suggestions that they should just give up trying to learn Danish.

Personally, I was told that my accent made it impossible to understand my order for a hot dog at a local sausage wagon.

Ethnic diversity

Denmark is no longer the all-white country it was 50 years ago.

People of color can be found at every level of the economic

spectrum: high-income specialists recruited by Denmark's biggest companies; middle-class people married to Danes; and less well-off refugees and their descendants, who often live in poor neighborhoods the Danish government insists on officially labelling as "ghettos."

Whatever their origin or income class, newcomers are expected to conform to Danish culture and contribute to the welfare state by working and paying taxes.

People who can do this are generally welcome, and people who can't are not.

The Danish government goes so far as to release statistics that show whether newcomers from specific countries are an economic plus or minus for Denmark. (US immigrants are in the "plus" category, as are newcomers from China and India, who are often skilled IT professionals.)

Most of the top levels of Danish politics and business are still populated by ethnic Danes, who make up 87% of the population.

There are, however, a few prominent politicians of diverse backgrounds. As younger generations move into the Danish workplace, there will probably be more diversity in positions of power.

What to wear in Denmark

Danish fashion is applauded in all the major style outlets, which cover the fabulous runway shows at Copenhagen Fashion Week.

In real life, though, Danes are not flashy dressers. They wear simple, dark clothing designed for the unpredictable Danish weather. Designer labels are seen as a little tacky for anyone past their teenage years. Quality is more important than trends.

And while it's a standard American opening remark to compliment someone's cool jacket or cute earrings, Danes will think it's odd if you comment on what they're wearing.

Basic business casual

A basic business casual wardrobe will take you through most of your appointments in Denmark. Blazer, sweater, shirt and trousers – all in subtle colors – and you're ready to go.

This outfit will make you look equal to the rest of your team, and equality is an essential part of Danish culture.

Anti-authoritarian dressing

A business contact recently told me about a young American woman visiting Denmark to make a presentation.

Eager to present herself as a powerful figure, she wore a chic suit and the highest heels she could manage.

It was the wrong signal. First of all, high heels are uncommon in Denmark; too much walking is required, and cobblestone streets don't play well with heels.

Secondly, the anti-authoritarian Danes don't like people who act or look like they're better than anyone else.

A simple outfit in fine fabrics, perhaps with a piece of statement jewelry, would have made a much better impression.

Don't be sloppy

There are also Americans who go too far in the other direction, showing up for work in sweatpants, surfer shorts, and shower shoes, or with their wet hair covered by a baseball cap.

This won't do. The Danes will think you are childish and unreliable.

Danes also don't share the American passion for sunglasses, in part because Denmark is grey and rainy for much of the year.

If for some reason you don't want to look American, put away your shades – and smile less often.

Gifts in Denmark

It is never necessary to bring a gift as part of doing business in Denmark. In fact, it may make your counterpart uncomfortable, since most companies have strict limits on what their employees can accept.

However, if you're invited to a private home in Denmark for dinner, it can be nice to bring a thoughtful gift for the host or hostess.

Specialty foods from your region

Specialty foods from your area of the US are always a hit: maple syrup, hot sauce, micro-brewed beer, local candy (but not chocolate: US chocolate is seen as deeply inferior to the European version.)

Don't bring fruit, cheeses, or meats, which you might not be able to get past customs.

No gag gifts or knick-knacks

Avoid gag gifts (*One can of pure New York City air!*) and knick-knacks. Danish homes are small and nobody has room for any clutter.

If your host has teenage children and you'd like to bring them a gift too, a jersey from your local sports team is usually welcome.

Danes and English

Danish children start learning English in school when they're six years old, and many pick up a few words and phrases in English before that through online videos and music.

That means that the majority of your Danish business partners will speak excellent English, with the occasional exception of older team members who came of age at a time when English was less important.

Still, they are not native speakers, and many learned from teachers who were not native speakers, so you'll still hear some occasional errors.

The most common ones have to do with irregular plurals ("My home has nice new **furnitures**") and subject-verb agreement ("**We are** very busy. **He are** very busy too.")

There's also a lot of confusion about the simple present tense versus the gerund (She **achieves** good results. She **is achieving** good results), a distinction that doesn't exist in Danish.

Direct translations

In general, however, Danes are very confident in English – sometimes too confident when it comes to directly translating their native language.

For example, it's very common for Danish colleagues to greet each other in the morning with *"Er du frisk?"*, which is a colloquial way of asking if they are ready for the day's professional challenges.

Translated directly, however, it comes out in English as "Are you fresh?", which sounds like an outtake from an anti-perspirant commercial.

UK vs US English

Danes have been taught that British English is the gold standard of the language and may insist that their corporate documents be in "UK English."

In practice, this generally means adding a "u" to color and replacing words like *realize* with *realise* along with a few grammatical doodles. (Some Danes seem to believe that there is a much greater distance between US and UK English – perhaps like the difference between Norwegian and Danish, another former colony/colonist relationship.)

If you're being hired in Denmark for something having to do with writing, they may ask if you can "write UK English." With a couple of hours of brushing up, you can.

Sorry, not sorry

In addition to having no direct translation for *please*, Danes are also much less likely to say "Excuse me" or "I'm sorry" than English speakers do.

(Danes do sometimes use the English word *sorry* for light transgressions – "I meant blueberries, not raspberries – *sorry*.")

But don't be surprised if someone pushing past you in a public place doesn't say anything at all.

In addition, Danes' flat tone and love of sarcasm can sometimes make them seem rude in English.

Learning Danish

Learning Danish is a must for people who want to make a life for themselves in Denmark, but it is not necessary for short business trips.

That said, even for short stays it can be useful to know the word for "thank you" – *tak* – plus "*hej*" (pronounced hi) to say hello and "*hej hej*" to say goodbye. You might also want to learn the word for your favorite beverage, whether it is *øl* (beer), *kaffe* (coffee) or *te* (tea.)

The beer is good in Denmark, but Danish cafés often

insist on serving hot tea and blended coffee in tall glasses that are painful to hold in your hands, at least until the beverage goes cold.

Some cultural differences just can't be explained.

Long-term stays in Denmark

Denmark is a lovely place to settle down for a while, or even permanently if you are ready to do battle with the immigration authorities.

Make sure you bring money. Denmark is an expensive place to live where you will own less stuff, but better stuff. There is no equivalent to the Dollar Store, Walmart, or Target in Denmark.

Over-the-counter medicines

Danes don't share Americans' passion for over-the-counter medicine. If you are a fan of Neosporin, NyQuil, Midol, Pepto-Bismol or Sinutab, bring some along. Generic Tylenol and Advil are easy to find in Denmark.

Pack extras of any personal care brands you can't live without. Items sent from the US (or anywhere else outside the EU) to Denmark require substantial postage plus withering customs and administration fees. Plan on at least $50 per item.

Bring lots of casual, warm, and waterproof clothing. You don't need huge polar jackets – Denmark rarely goes below 0 on the Fahrenheit scale – but halter tops and suede loafers will see very little service.

An apartment in Denmark

If you rent an apartment in Denmark, be aware that it will need to be spotless, repainted, and sometimes refloored when you return it. Take time-stamped photos on the day you move in to avoid arguments later.

Many urban apartments do not have bathtubs, only showers. In some cases, you will need to buy your own refrigerator and washer-dryer for a rental apartment.

Europe uses a different electrical current than the US, so leave your blenders, mixers, and hairdryers at home unless you want to constantly use them with a converter, which is a pain and a fire hazard.

Bedding systems are different, too; mattresses are thinner and there are no flat sheets.

Kitchen garbage disposals do not exist in Denmark. Instead, many communities have specific programs to pick up organic waste, which is carefully separated from plastic, metal, paper, and glass.

Air conditioning is unusual in Denmark, because the weather is rarely hot enough to require it. You can always open a window, but the windows have no screens.

Religious services

If you're a Christian and want to go to services during your time in Denmark, seek out an international church. Danish state churches, which are supported by a voluntary tax, are very quiet and usually poorly attended.

There are very small Jewish and Hindu communities in Denmark, and a large Muslim community. Muslims make up roughly 6% of the Danish population, and there are several new and attractive mosques financed from abroad.

Medical care in Denmark

Anyone with legal residence in Denmark is entitled to tax-financed Danish medical care. You will be asked to choose a doctor shortly after you arrive, selecting from a list of general practitioners close to your home address.

Ask your colleagues for recommendations; alternately, you may get some good tips from the many Facebook groups for internationals living in Denmark.

Dentistry for adults and many types of psychological care are not covered by the public system, so you'll have to pay for those services out of pocket if you need them.

Annual physicals are uncommon, and testing is less extensive. Mammograms start at age 50, for example, instead of age 40 as in much of the US.

In addition, some people of Asian or African descent living in Denmark have told me that ethnic Danish doctors aren't always familiar with medical conditions that are specific to people of color, such as sickle cell anaemia.

Finding a doctor who shares your ethnicity isn't always possible, particularly outside of the big cities.

You may need to get aggressive about your care, insisting on a second opinion, if you suspect that your doctor isn't giving you the right advice.

The Executive Summary: Top things to remember

Thanks for reading this far in the book. Here are a few points to remember when doing business in Denmark.

* * *

Danish culture is based on authenticity and trust. Don't BS anybody, and never promise anything you cannot deliver in full. Trust is the default – you are granted it, you don't have to earn it – but once lost, it is almost impossible to get back.

* * *

Denmark is an anti-authoritarian culture, so anyone who walks in acting like a big cheese will be resented and mocked. Your job title or place in the hierarchy isn't particularly important to your Danish team. They are practical people interested in what you can deliver.

* * *

For Danes, personal time outside work is very important. Don't expect your team to stay extra hours unless there's an urgent deadline, don't schedule meetings after 3pm, and be careful to avoid common vacation periods when you schedule product launches. When it comes to your team members, focus on the work produced, not the time served.

* * *

Danes resent micromanagement. They feel that if you've hired them to do a job, you should get out of the way and let them do it. The Danish "flat hierarchy" with fewer middle managers means you often don't have the personnel to keep constant watch on your team anyway. Keep in mind that because Denmark is less litigious than the US, some record-keeping can be unnecessary.

* * *

Danes have a great love for free speech and can be extremely direct, sometimes to the point of seeming rude. Occasionally, they will say uncomfortable things and then insist this was only an example of "Danish humor." At any rate, expect a great deal of sarcasm, and don't assume it is always negativity.

* * *

Cocooned in the welfare state, Danes may not understand

why Americans are so competitive and sometimes jumpy. Some of your Danish colleagues may seem unambitious, but that's because they have everything they want in life – a good job, a nice home, and plenty of free time. They will still be ambitious for their products and product quality.

* * *

Most Americans have been conditioned not to go around the world saying their country is the best of all possible countries, but Danes have no such reservations. They are quite proud of their culture and their system and are not particularly receptive to any kind of constructive criticism.

* * *

Denmark is a small, gentle, well-kept and very pretty country. Make sure to schedule some time away from business events to explore its beautiful beaches, wonderful museums, and tiny villages full of houses with straw roofs.

Appendix: A few notes on Danish history

Many books on business culture contain long, droning sections on a country's history, which might be exactly the kind of thing you thought you'd escape by choosing a business degree.

This is a short book, so here are some very short points about Danish history that might come up in business conversation.

* * *

The Vikings were in action from roughly 800 to 1100 AD. Clever traders and inventors who came up with the solar compass, boat keel, and other innovations having to do with their line of work, the Vikings were the first Europeans to visit North America.

Because many Vikings settled down in England after their raids, some English words are similar to words in modern Danish. The English word sky, for example, mimics *sky*, the Danish word for cloud.

* * *

Denmark once had an empire that included all of Norway, Iceland, northern Germany, and the southern half of Sweden. It shrank bit by bit over the centuries, and the final blow was a crushing defeat by the Germans in 1864.

This loss was heartbreaking to the Danes, and it is often referenced in popular culture.

It was a lesson on how to manage defeat in a graceful way, which comes in handy when Denmark competes at international sporting events.

* * *

One thing that comes up less often in popular culture is Denmark's role in the Atlantic slave trade.

Tens of thousands of enslaved Africans were brought from what is now Ghana to the Danish West Indies before slavery was abolished there in 1848.

Denmark sold these territories to the US in 1917 for a modest $25 million, and you may know them as the US Virgin Islands.

* * *

From 1880 to 1920, more than 350,000 Danes – about 15% of the total population – left Denmark for the US, settling primarily in Wisconsin, Minnesota, Iowa, and the Pacific Northwest.

Denmark was experiencing a population explosion at the time, and there was simply not enough farmland to go around.

The parts of the US to which they moved, usually to work as farmers, resemble Denmark in terrain and climate.

* * *

The country's World War II experience was a complicated one. When Denmark was invaded by the Germans in 1940, the small country's leaders realized that they would not be able to fight the Nazis – who were then at the peak of their power – and surrendered quickly.

Denmark was occupied for five years, although the Danes did a good job of helping many Jews escape to neutral Sweden.

While a Danish resistance movement sabotaged the occupying German forces, a few thousand Danes also volunteered to fight on the German side.

The 1960s and 1970s were a time of change in Denmark. The welfare state grew quickly. Hundreds of day care centers, hospitals, schools, and nursing homes were built, and many social and class barriers broke down.

Even the Danish language changed noticeably, with the formal version of "you" – familiar to speakers of French, Spanish, and German – mostly disappearing.

In 1967, Denmark became the first country in the world to legalize pornography, which led to a thriving trade in X-rated films and magazines.

At the same time, a strong feminist movement emerged, which means you'll probably never hear a cat call in Denmark unless it comes from a foreigner.

It was also during these decades that Denmark began inviting "guest workers" from Turkey to work in Danish industry, its first step into non-European immigration.

Today, one out of five children born in Denmark has at least one parent who is not an ethnic Dane.

About the Author

Kay Xander Mellish is a speaker, writer, and cultural coach based in Copenhagen, Denmark.

A native of Wauwatosa, Wisconsin, Kay studied journalism and art history at New York University. She worked for several US Fortune 500 companies including units of Disney, News Corp., and Time-Warner before moving to Denmark, where she was employed by Carlsberg and Danske Bank.

This is Kay's fifth book, and a companion volume to her previous book, *Working with Americans: Tips for Danes.*

Kay's first book, *How to Live in Denmark: An entertaining guide for newcomers and their Danish friends*, was based on her long-running podcast and is for sale at Denmark's National Museum.

Kay's book *How to Work in Denmark: Tips on succeeding at work and understanding your Danish boss* has been ordered in bulk by several large Danish companies for distribution to their newly-arrived international specialists.

You can bulk order copies of Kay's books or book Kay for consulting or speeches at www.kxmgroup.dk.

A Fun Flip Book

WORKING WITH AMERICANS / WORKING WITH DANES

KAY XANDER MELLISH

Publisher – BoD Copenhagen, Denmark
Printer – BoD Norderstedt, Germany
ISBN 978-87-4302-813-0

WORKING WITH AMERICANS

TIPS FOR DANES

AN ENTERTAINING GUIDE TO BUSINESS CO-OPERATION

KAY XANDER MELLISH

For May 5 and July 4

Introduction

As an American who has lived in Denmark for more than 10 years, I'm often asked by my Danish clients for tips on how to work better with their American colleagues.

It's usually the smartest people in the organization who ask the question. Others seem to assume that because they speak great English and have watched every episode of their favorite US TV series that they have a handle on the American culture and way of doing business.

As the great American composer George Gershwin once titled a song, *it ain't necessarily so.*

Shaped by location and history

Denmark and the US are both wonderful countries, yet each has been shaped by its own location and history.

Denmark's tradition of social welfare has grown out of centuries of farmers and fishermen trying to help each other survive the punishing Nordic climate.

American confidence and can-do spirit is a result of generations of immigrants gutsy enough to leave their home countries to try something new.

More in common

That said, the countries have more in common than they have differences.

Both are passionate about free speech and self-determination. Neither one has much patience for formalities. Both enjoy a good business deal.

As a citizen of both countries, I hope this book helps Danes and Americans work together even more successfully.

Kay Xander Mellish

Copenhagen, Summer 2019

Why the US is a great place to do business

Most Danes have been exposed to American culture since childhood, and some feel they know it as instinctively as they know their own.

Yet it's hard for anyone who doesn't live in the US to appreciate how diverse, chaotic, and simply *big* the place is. One Danish businessman said he first got the message when he drove his large American rental car onto an interstate highway in Kansas and his GPS told him "Next turn in 250 miles."

(That's 400 kilometers, for people not well-versed in the convoluted US measurement system.)

Fifty personalities – and more

Unlike most European countries, which are for better or worse nations centered around a capitol city, the United States is fifty different states with fifty different personalities.

Some states even have more than one personality – Northern California, for example, has an entirely different vibe than Southern California, and upstate New York has none of the buzz or hype of New York City.

Laws are different in every state, so what is legal and openly sold in one state, such as cannabis or cannabis products, can land you in jail in another.

Localities also make their own rules and regulations: for example, several cities in California have banned plastic drinking straws and forks.

And every state and locality has its own tax structure, which is why sales tax (MOMS) is *added* to the listed price in the US, not included in it. If you take a $10 item to the cash register in Seattle it will cost you $11.10, but in nearby Spokane, it will be $10.89, and only $10 in the next-door state of Oregon, which has no sales tax at all.

Danes focus on what they know

Failing to understand the diversity of the US is one of the biggest mistakes Danes make when approaching the country for business. There is no guarantee that a product that is a smash in Utah will be of any interest at all in Kentucky.

Danes also tend to focus on areas they know from their vacations in the US or the media: Los Angeles, Manhattan, maybe Miami or Boston.

But much of the economic and population growth in the US is taking place in cities that are less well known in Denmark.

San Antonio, Texas; Phoenix, Arizona; and Jacksonville, Florida all have bigger populations than the more famous cities of San Francisco, Seattle, or Denver.

Understanding American diversity

Another surprise for Danes can be the extreme diversity of the US population. Despite a great deal of rhetoric about the opening and closing of borders, the US has been undergoing an immigration boom since the 1990s. One out of eight US residents was born someplace else.

The upside of this diversity is a youthful energy and an unending supply of new ideas and fresh viewpoints; the downside is that since everyone is coming from a slightly different perspective, Americans lack the automatic understanding and trust of each other that Danes take for granted.

That's why smiles and small talk are so important. Americans from wildly different backgrounds need to establish that they're on the same page for at least as long as it takes to address the matter at hand.

It also means there is a thicket of rules and regulations to make sure everyone is treated equally.

Danes who like to do business on impulse and instinct

may find themselves tearing their hair out as they try to comply with the US Equal Opportunity laws.

Putting aside stereotypes

In addition to nixing stereotypes about specific types of people, you will need to discard stereotypes about the US as a whole, many of them nurtured by the Danish media.

Gun ownership is not universal, the majority of Americans are not wildly obese, and every highway does not look like that one open road in Arizona that seems to be the setting for dozens of on-the-road Danish TV advertisements.

The good news is that you won't have to worry about American stereotypes of Denmark: they generally don't have any, except for a persistent tendency to confuse Denmark with the Netherlands and tell you how much they'd like to visit Amsterdam.

(Yes, Americans are bad at European geography, but be honest: could you really pinpoint the states of North Carolina, North Dakota, and New Hampshire on a map and explain their cultural differences?)

Doing business in the US

The US is a good place to do business. Americans enjoy working – in fact, they get much of their self-esteem from working – and people are generally open, helpful, and friendly, even if it is the kind of transitory friendliness that Danes sometimes feel is *not real*.

It may not be real, but it is pleasant, and if you spend some time in the US then return to Denmark, you may miss it.

Meanwhile, the size and wealth of the American market offers enormous rewards for a company with a good product, good marketing, and good luck.

High risk, high reward

The American market – and the American way of life in general – is *high risk, high reward*. Much more than in Denmark, there is a widespread acceptance that there are winners and losers in life.

But it's considered OK to fail, and sometimes even to tell people how far down you were and how you used grit and determination to crawl back up again.

You were only *failing forward*, as the popular self-help expression goes.

For Danes brought up on safety, equality, and contentment, this nonstop instability can seem like life on a rollercoaster.

The most important advice

The most important piece of advice I can give a Dane seeking to do business in the US is this: treat it like a foreign country.

Danes' familiarity with American culture can sometimes

trick them into thinking that the US is just a larger, more colorful Denmark with bigger cars.

It is not. US business culture is full of quirks and cultural traps, and you need to study that culture and proceed cautiously, just like you would if you were doing business in Asia, Africa, or Latin America.

The good news is that America is such a diverse place that you won't be the only newcomer feeling your way along in an unfamiliar culture.

The country is set up to welcome new people, which it has been absorbing bit by bit since the first humans walked across the Bering Strait from Asia about 20,000 years ago.

Welcome to America!

The enthusiasm gap and why you will have to act excited to succeed in the US

Denmark is a flat country, I often tell newcomers at my *How to Live in Denmark* speeches, and when you live and work here your tone and emotions should be flat as well.

No wild gesturing or, as the Danes call them, "big arm movements." No dramatic statements about right and wrong. No losing your temper and raising your voice.

For Danes, being calm and in control is a sign of being a mature adult.

But for emotional exhibitionists like the Americans, this quiet composure can give the impression you are unenthusiastic, uninterested, or even bored.

Exclamation points mean excitement

If you've received emails or even marketing materials

from your US colleagues, you've probably already realized that they are fond of using the exclamation point.

One marketing director from a Danish company told me he went through the text and edited out every single one of them. "They sound like shouting," he told his American employees.

The Americans were distressed. "Exclamation points represent excitement!" they said. "They give the text energy! They tell customers that we really believe in our product."

A cultural difference you must adapt to

Enthusiasm, high energy, and positivity is just part of the fuel Americans need to succeed in an often merciless competitive environment.

It is one of those cultural differences you will have to surrender to if you hope to be successful in the US – just like you would have to learn the intricacies of hierarchy if you were working in Asia.

To do well in the US, you will have to at least pretend to be as energetic and eager as the Americans you work with.

Titles, hierarchy, and why they matter to Americans

Many Danish managers who come to the US look forward to teaching Americans about the Danish flat hierarchy.

They are proud of this egalitarian approach and are sure it will be a hit in the country where, as the Declaration of Independence put it, "all men are created equal."

But it isn't a hit, because Americans don't really want to be equal. They want to compete, and if all possible they want to win.

Competition begins in childhood

Growing up in high-security social welfare state like Denmark, it is hard to imagine the lifelong race-to-the-top that begins when American children barely know their own names.

Concerned American parents start teaching their children to read as early as age 3, and strategize to get access to the best possible school for their child to begin around 5 or 6.

Wealthy parents undergo interviews to get their darlings into the most prestigious private school; middle-class parents choose their homes based on the quality of local public schools; poor parents join lotteries for high-quality "magnet" schools or send their kids to safe and orderly Catholic schools even if they aren't religious.

The college admissions race

In their teenage years, kids spend an enormous amount of time preparing for the SATs, the national standardized test many universities use for admission, and getting involved in the kind of extra-curricular activities that might impress college admissions officers.

The idea is to get into the best possible university with the maximum amount of financial aid, then to graduate near the top of your class, get a great first job (or start a company) right out of school and begin a life of success upon success.

The job title is a payoff for lifetime striving

An impressive job title is a sign of this success, and indicates that all the hard work has paid off.

Not only will the title's owner hold it close to his heart,

but so will his parents ("*My son is the CFO of a large B2B software company*") plus any people he might be interested in dating ("*Let me introduce you to a guy I know. He's an executive.*")

The naïve newly-arrived Danish manager who announces that from now on, everyone will be equal and titles don't matter rips away a little piece of this American striver's soul.

Titles don't always indicate real power

That said, titles aren't always reflective of how much power an employee has within the organization, particularly nebulous titles like "Vice President", which are often given out instead of a raise.

If you're trying to figure out who in a partner organization has the power to make things happen or the ability to sign on the dotted line, look for factors like headcount responsibility or the importance of their department to the company's overall strategy.

The celebrity boss, and why Americans want to "hitch their wagon to a star"

To a Dane, a charismatic American boss may come across as flashy, flakey, and a bit manipulative.

But to an American, the standard consensus-seeking Danish boss may seem passive and directionless.

An ambitious American employee wants an energetic, inspirational boss that can inspire her and take her career to the next level.

The expression "hitch your wagon to a star" is an old one, but indicates a hunger to attach yourself to a more established, stronger figure who can take you aloft with them, like a kite.

Cheerleaders and drill sergeants

Americans see great bosses as motivators, cheerleaders, and drill sergeants, optimizing and energizing their teams to get the best performance out of every member.

This is why Americans buy books and watch movies about charismatic business leaders – from Steve Jobs to Donald Trump to Jay-Z to millennial "Girlboss" Sophia Amoruso.

A boss is a star, and employees revolve around her like planets revolve around the sun.

So much for consensus

This status-based solar system means it is the boss who makes decisions and is ultimately accountable for those decisions.

She may ask for input from her team, but it's quite common to see a boss make a quick decision without consulting anyone at all.

If the decision turns out to be wrong, many employees will silently un-hitch their wagons and slink away, although others will remain at the boss' side until the cycle of business brings her back to the top again.

Very few American bosses are such a big failure that they don't get a second chance, or even a third or fourth.

"How are you?" Small talk and how to do it

One perennial complaint of Danes who do business with Americans is the necessity of small talk.

Why, they ask again and again, do Americans say, *How are you doing?* when they really don't want to know how I am doing?

My response is always this: *How are you doing?* is not a question, it is a greeting, much like *Go' morgen* or *Go' weekend*.

When you say *Go' morgen*, nobody wants to hear that it is not in fact a good morning, that you ran out of cornflakes and the bus was late and your dog threw up all over the carpet last night so the living room smells awful.

All they want to hear is *Go' morgen* in return.

Tips for how to respond

That said, I do teach Danes how to respond to "How are you doing?" or similar questions like "How was your weekend?" or "How was your flight?"

My advice is always to respond with a single, positive detail.

How are you? *Great. I'm enjoying this weather.*

How was your weekend? *Wonderful. Spent some time with family, went for a walk with the kids.*

How was your flight? *Smooth and on time. I watched some movies I've been wanting to see for ages.*

One simple personal detail lets your associate get to know you a bit better, and understand that you are not a crazy foreigner or a robot.

Now you can ask a polite return question – "And how are *you* doing?" – get a one-line answer, then move on to business.

Remember that detail should always be positive. If you offer a negative detail, the Americans will try to fix the problem for you. Your flight was delayed, you got nothing to eat? *Oh no, let me get you a sandwich.*

Longer conversations

You may find yourself at an informal dinner with colleagues you don't know well, or with their spouses, who are sometimes included in business entertaining.

How can you fill the evening with small talk that won't cause offense?

Asking about your conversational partner's connection to the location is always a good conversation starter. You might ask, *Did you grow up here in Oklahoma?*

The odds are likely that they did not. Americans move around a lot. You can then ask about the differences between where they used to live and where they live now.

That said, it is considered poor form to ask an American with an accent *Where do you **really** come from?* Assume that everyone is 100% American born and bred unless they inform you otherwise.

College days

Where they went to university is also something Americans like to talk about, because to some extent it defines a graduate for the rest of his or her life.

Someone who went to University of Michigan thinks of himself as an entirely different type of human than someone who went to, say, Michigan State University.

Let Americans talk about the school where they spent their youth (and perhaps about its sports teams) and they will be happy for hours.

TV shows, sports teams, and kids

You can also enquire about your conversational partner's favorite movies, TV shows, and professional sports teams.

Pets are a good conversational topic too – some people call pets their "fur babies."

If the conversation involves actual offspring, you may find that your American associates brag about their kids' achievements in a way you would never think to do in Denmark.

Their kids are on the first level of the great American meritocracy race, so it's extremely important that they are doing well at their piano lessons and are leaders in the Scouts and just won a surfing award.

If you respond by explaining that your children back in Denmark are basically just kids being kids, Americans may secretly wonder if perhaps they aren't a bit disappointing to you.

Conversation topics to avoid

As an American in Denmark, it has been my experience that many Danes are saving up things they really want to "tell an American."

They are unhappy with some aspect of American politics or history and want to make sure they are heard by somebody, even somebody who can't do anything about their complaint.

This is a poor tactic for business small talk.

Americans know their country is in no way perfect, and there are many things they would like to change themselves.

Still, the homelessness crisis or the legacy of slavery is not something they usually want to discuss with someone they have just met over a meal, any more than you would want to have a light chat about the "stolen generation" in Greenland or *Frikorps Danmark*'s role in the Waffen SS. It makes for strained dinner table conversation.

Once you get to know an American well, he or she may be open to a discussion of serious issues. But usually not right away.

In general, avoiding politics during small talk is a very good idea.

You may believe that there is only one sensible way to vote in the US, but statistics will show that about half of Americans voted differently, and you can't easily tell who they are.

Danish directness vs American "positive face"

When I speak to Danes about their way of communicating, I often show a photo of a George Jensen silver bowl, the modernist "Bloom" that can be found in thousands of Danish homes.

This lovely bowl has elegant, simple lines and no ornamentation. Nothing is there that is unneeded.

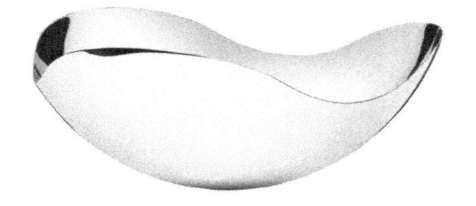

It's a good metaphor for the way Danes like to talk to each other: simple, direct, no filter. Openness and complete honesty, they believe, is the best way to get things done.

The Americans receiving that communication aren't so sure.

Directness in a monoculture

Like so many other things about life in Denmark, Danes' direct and sometimes harsh way of speaking to each other is a benefit of a monoculture.

When everyone around you has a similar upbringing and similar values, you can say what you mean without putting it into context and know that your listener will not take it as a personal insult.

In a multicultural society like the United States, a little more contextualizing (you could call it padding) is necessary.

This is in line with anthropologists' findings that diverse societies smile more: a smile is a way of building up trust with a stranger. Americans smile relentlessly and spend an enormous amount of money caring for and beautifying their teeth.

Encouraging little expressions

That means when you work with Americans, your direct message will have to be proceeded by encouraging little expressions that help build a pleasant atmosphere.

This is "positive face", your acknowledgement that your American employee or counterpart is indeed a very nice person who is doing his or her best to shine at the business at hand.

It can seem exasperating to Danes, but it is what Americans expect, and if you go right to the meat of the matter – particularly if you are delivering a critique – you will seem brusque and even cruel.

Language tricks

Part of sounding more supportive is a trick of language: the conditional (*I would like you to sell more widgets*) is seen as softer and more polite than the direct present tense (*I want you to sell more widgets*).

There are also some expressions you can use to kindly push your American colleagues in the direction you would like them to go.

If you're waiting for some overdue test results, for example, you might say:

- *Just a reminder – we're waiting for those test results. When will they be ready?*
- *I'm looking forward to the test results. Will they be ready by Friday?*
- *I wanted to quickly follow up. How far along are the test results?*

Sometimes, of course, you need to be a bit more insistent. If your request is less of a push and more than a demand, try formulations like:

- *I'm afraid I need those test results today. What time will I have them?*

- *I need those test results ASAP. Please have them for me by the end of business today.*
- *Getting the test results is my top priority today. Please make that happen.*

A few Danes have told me that they feel the word "please" (a word that does not exist in Danish) makes them look weak and pleading, instead of being in command of the situation.

In fact, the opposite is true. Extreme politeness in English is a sign of power, as you'll experience if an American traffic cop says *Sir, please get out of the car and put your hands on the roof.*

This is a direct order, nicely wrapped in a bit of courtesy.

Use numbers to express urgency

US businesses love to measure their employees, so those employees are accustomed to hearing priorities expressed as numbers.

You can use this when communicating with your American colleagues. "Don't spend too much time on this," you might say about a project. "For me, it's a 4 on a scale of 10."

Alternately, you can use numbers to express urgency. "On a scale of 10, this is an 11," you might say. "Please get it done today."

The American litigation monster and what it means for you

I live in a complex near Copenhagen with about 115 apartments, and one hot summer our tenants' association declared it was going to put up a swimming pool.

Not a small inflatable pool that could be packed away at the end of the day, but a large, above-ground, hard-sided pool that would sit proudly in our central yard and be up all summer.

As a keen swimmer, this sounded great, but as an American, I was terrified by the safety and legal implications.

"You can't just leave an open pool up with no fence and no lifeguard," I said. "What happens if someone goes in there late at night and drowns? It would be terrible for their family and we could be sued for everything we've got."

My Danish neighbors thought I was being a kill-joy. "We'll just keep an eye on it," they said. "It will be fine."

Det skal nok gå. You could see it as Danish confidence or Danish carelessness.

But for whatever reason, that pool never was put up.

Fear of lawsuits is constant

When I first arrived in Denmark, I remember being shocked at traditions that could make an American liabilities lawyer rich.

Whether it was bonfires at kindergartens, open grills of hot coals to warm your hands at Tivoli, or drunken high-school graduates riding on open-top trucks, I couldn't help thinking about how a stupid or careless person might injure himself and sue.

American businesses think about this all the time, since they have two things on their mind: how to stay in business at a profit, and how to avoid litigation, since the second can make the first impossible. Every business decision, every product development or marketing technique, every hiring and every firing, has to be looked at through the lens of *Can we be sued for this?*

This is why many American products come with ridiculous legal disclaimers (*Do not use this toothpaste in your eyes*) and why most US contracts are long and full of strange clauses.

Such contracts are not written to be understood. They are written so they cannot be misunderstood.

Social events and lawsuits

Even social events take place in the shadow of possible litigation.

This is why Americans have trouble understanding the amount of alcohol served at Danish office parties. An American boss has to keep in mind that if someone misbehaves at or on the way home from one of these parties, the company may be held liable.

And if the boss herself has one too many cocktails and makes a smart remark about an employee's anatomy or ethnicity, she could end up in trouble with HR at best, and with a career-ending lawsuit at worst.

Better to stay sober and go home early, or stage the party at a local bar where people buy their own drinks and are therefore responsible for what they do afterwards. (The bar, however, can still be held liable in some cases.)

Disabilities and lawsuits

Like the *Forskelsbehandlingsloven* in Denmark, the Americans with Disabilities Act prohibits discrimination based on disability, and requires companies to make "reasonable accommodation" for disabled employees and make all company spaces accessible to people with disabilities.

This is why most public spaces in the US have toilet stalls large enough for a wheelchair user to maneuver in, and why every hotel pool has a small motorized dunking chair so that disabled guests can take a dip if they choose.

Unlike Denmark, the US is home to a small army of professional litigants armed with rulers who can be counted on to measure your tables, bathroom sinks, and entrance options to make sure they comply.

You may be required to make your non-public office space compliant for workers with disabilities as well. And the definition of disabilities can be surprising. Severe obesity is one of them, for example.

Seek guidance on this from your new best friend – your lawyer.

Sexual harassment and hostile workplaces

It goes without saying that you should not require sexual favors as a condition of employment, and it's a good idea to avoid sexual jokes or any touching at all with employees of the opposite gender, or of the same gender if you are gay.

This collides with the infuriating American habit of hugging instead of shaking hands, but that's just the way it goes.

Dating an employee is also a highway to hell in a legal sense. No matter how lonely you are, far from home, try to avoid it.

In addition to avoiding sexual harassment yourself, you are required to be on the lookout for and take action against any of your staff who may be behaving badly. Otherwise, the lawsuits and bad publicity will rebound on the company and on you.

The same is true if you have any employees being mocked for their skin color, gender, religion, sexuality, or disability, which can create what the lawyers call a "hostile work environment."

In such cases you must take immediate action, usually with a written warning for first-time offenders.

The Danish way of doing things – *"everyone should be able to take a joke, and everyone has to learn to make fun of themselves"* – does not apply in the hyper-litigious United States.

If you think you might have a legal problem, it's always a good idea to ask for legal advice *before* instead of *after* the other side approaches their lawyer. It's better to act too early than too late.

Dining out and the secrets of tipping culture

The "three-martini" lunch in a fine restaurant was once the standard for US corporate entertaining, but it is now rare. Many employees, including some executives, eat at their desks. Others grab a quick bite at a fast-casual or takeout place.

Even so, inviting a contact or a potential client to lunch or dinner in a restaurant is an excellent way to get a bit of distraction-free face time.

Dining out is nothing special

Dining out in the US is not a special occasion the way it often is in Denmark.

But it also means that you may feel you are being hurried through the meal and hustled out the door. For restaurant owners, margins are thin and it is important to turn over tables to new customers.

If you are dining at a place with a server, you may be annoyed by the server's repeated interruptions asking if you would like anything else, or if you are interested in dessert.

The server is also a businesswoman: under direction from the management, she is trying to increase your total bill and thereby increase her tip.

Tipping culture and why it survives

Danes tend to be exasperated by American tipping culture.

Why, they ask, can't these servers just be paid a living wage, and have that wage be incorporated into the menu prices?

Some servers would probably agree with you, but others would not, because a skilled server collecting tips can make a lot more than a living wage.

If business is good at a high-end restaurant or busy bar, a server might be able to survive by working as little as three nights a week, leaving the rest of her time free to audition for acting roles, attend university, or run a side business.

A recent initiative by a high-end New York restaurant group to eliminate tipping collapsed when 30-40% of its experienced servers quit, complaining that they were not getting the extra income from tips during high-volume hours.

The going rate for tipping

Currently, a 20% tip is the going rate for satisfactory service, although if your server went out of his way for you (such as mopping up an embarrassing table spill and bringing you a fresh bowl of soup), 25% is appreciated.

Do not go below 15%, which is what the American tax authorities generally expect a server to receive. If you do, he may end up paying taxes on money he didn't get, which means he will have actually lost money by serving you.

Should the food or the service be so terrible that you feel resentful about leaving anything at all, have a polite chat with the restaurant manager, who may give you a portion of your meal for free. (And if he does, you should still tip based on the full value of the meal.)

Tipping* is particularly important if you are dining with American business contacts. They know that Europeans often undertip, and are occasionally so embarrassed that they sneak back to tip the server properly.

Big portions in American restaurants

Another thing that often upsets Danes is the very large portions in American restaurants. *Who needs so much food?* they ask themselves. *No wonder this country has an obesity problem.*

Big portions are partly a competitive necessity: if every other restaurant nearby is serving generous portions,

no restaurant wants to be the one that comes up short. Besides, food ingredients are relatively cheap in the US, compared to other restaurant expenses like labor, utilities, rent, and taxes.

Also, it is considered completely OK to take home leftover food from a restaurant and use it for a second meal, or even two meals.

Danes tend to have a visceral disgust for this idea of taking home food, which always surprises me because they are usually so efficient about avoiding waste.

Do as you please in the US, but no server will be offended if you ask him to kindly "wrap this up" to take home. (The term "doggy bag" is outdated; everyone knows it is probably you, not your dog, who will be enjoying the leftovers.)

Drinking at American restaurants

Very few adult American business people drink alcohol with the gusto of their Danish counterparts.

Getting drunk – really, really drunk – is seen as the territory of university students and alcoholics.

Many Americans don't drink for religious reasons, health reasons, because they have a personal or family history of addiction, or because they are trying to get pregnant. Others will avoid alcohol because they need to drive home.

Never encourage your American associate to drink or drink more, and don't be offended if they do not drink at all.

Put away your toothpick

The Danish habit of taking a toothpick after a shared meal and doing a full dental cleaning at the table (often behind a strategically placed hand) is a no-go in the US, and probably in many other places as well.

Bring a toothbrush and stop by the restroom on the way out if your dental hygiene is urgent.

*Tipping is always an inexact science, but the best way to handle it is to carry a large wad of $1 and $5 dollar bills and to be ready to share them generously.

Give a bartender a generous tip – $5, $10, or $20, depending on the size of your order – on the very first round of drinks and you can be assured of excellent service all night.

It's always better to tip with cash than credit cards, because you can then be more confident that it goes to the person providing you service and not his employer.

Many Americans finance university for their children (or themselves) with tips received from people like you.

Why you are getting CC'd on so many emails

One of the top complaints I hear from Danish bosses working with Americans is the large number of "CC" emails they receive. "Why do they CC me on everything?" the Danes ask. "I don't really need to know all this stuff."

Some of those CC's are no doubt cover-your-butt maneuvers (*I CC'd my boss about this, so if it all goes wrong it's not my fault*) but the vast majority are because their American bosses really did want to know all this stuff.

Staying in the loop

American bosses are obsessed with staying "in the loop" and feel the need to be on top of what's going on in their teams at all times.

This isn't always because they love micro-managing. The fearsome US legal machine requires them to know

everything about possible defects in their product as well as any bias or harassment on their team.

The busily CC'ing American employees are creating a "paper trail" in case of a future lawsuit.

Content-free emails

You may find that the emails you receive from your US-based managers contain little direct information, and certainly no direct responses to difficult questions asked.

This is because many American managers can picture their emails being read out in a court of law.

If you want to get the real scoop on a difficult matter, telephone your manager at a time when she will have the office to herself.

Getting the real truth at lunch

Even better, arrange a business lunch in a nice restaurant. Relax during the meal and enjoy light topics. Then, before dessert comes, drop the bomb: *Why isn't our sales team performing? Is it their team leader's fault, or have we hired the wrong customer-facing people?*

Away from prying eyes and recording devices, your manager can say what she really thinks.

She knows perfectly well that if she's ever asked to repeat in court what she's telling you now, she can say that she "doesn't recall" sharing it with you.

Hiring and firing Americans without getting sued

Let me start off this chapter by noting that I am not an attorney, and you should probably get one if not several before you begin taking on American employees.

Anyway, here is my non-legal opinion: hiring and firing is one of the top headaches for Danes who do business in the US.

'Cultural fit' vs 'Protected class'

Danes are used to hiring whomever they want – in particular, whichever applicant seems like the best "cultural fit".

If that person isn't a fit after all, or if conditions change and the business needs different or fewer employees, they let that person go.

That's a recipe for a lifetime of lawsuits in the US, where

there are very strong protections to ensure that no one is being hired (or not being hired) or fired (or not being fired) because of their race, religion, gender, national origin, age, sexuality, gender identity, or disability.

These are the "protected classes" in the US.

Get out the rulebook for job interviews

Perhaps you are holding interviews and declined to hire someone in one of the protected classes because they were wrong for the job or showed up late and seemed to have no idea what job they were applying for.

You could still be required to show that this person was not rejected because they are in a protected class.

That means that when it comes to interviews, you'll have to throw Danish flexibility out the window and do things by a strict American HR handbook designed to avoid lawsuits, including those from serial litigants who make a living suing unfortunate businesses.

An acquaintance of mine was targeted by this type of person, who claimed she had been turned down for a job because she was deaf. Amazingly, my acquaintance's small business already had two deaf employees, so the lawsuit was thrown out of court. But my acquaintance still had to pay substantial legal fees.

Firing an American employee

Firing an employee in the US is an even more delicate

situation with the potential for lawsuits.

Your attorney will give you the specifics, but a good point of departure is to keep excellent records.

If Employee A is in a protected class but is producing such poor results that she needs to be fired, you may be asked in court for records that prove this.

Those records will also need to show the results of her colleagues: was Employee B, who is not in a protected class, really doing all that better? Why was Employee A fired and not Employee B?

In the Danish seat-of-your-pants business style, keeping records like this may seem like a colossal waste of time. And it is. But it is the price of hiring people in the US.

Get the right vocabulary

Fyret in Danish can mean an employee terminated for any reason, but in American English, *fired* means the employee has been shown the door because of very bad behavior.

Given the legal tiptoeing around employment situations that's required in the US, it's usually better to say that someone is "no longer with the company" or has "moved on."

If you need to emphasize that the decision was made on your side (a dangerous vanity in most cases), you could say

that the employee was "let go".

When large numbers of people lose their jobs through no fault of their own but because of changes in business conditions, the usual term is that they were "laid off".

American diversity and the Danish businessperson

The US is no longer the mostly white and black populace you might have seen in old movies on Danish TV.

The greatest number of immigrants to the US now come from Asia, but there are also plenty who originate from Latin America, the Caribbean, Africa, and the Middle East.

Most people get along pretty well, although residential neighborhoods are often segregated as people choose to live near people like themselves.

But restaurants, shopping malls, and movie theaters tend to attract mixed groups, and you will see the full rainbow of American diversity on the road and on mass transit.

Dealing with racial friction

Occasionally, of course, there is friction, and sometimes the most innocent of disagreements, like an argument over a parking space, can take on a racial element if the two participants come from different backgrounds.

If this happens to you, try to take the high road and stay focused on the matter at hand, although the other party may not necessarily do so.

(In case you haven't heard it yet, "cracker" is the term of racial disparagement for light-skinned people of European origin. "Becky" or "Karen" is a negative term for light-skinned women.)

Should you get involved in this type of disagreement, it's a good idea to behave as if you are being recorded on video for all your friends and business associates to see. You often are.

Avoiding hurt feelings

As a foreigner, you may not be familiar with all the hurtful stereotypes that have been part of the American past in order to avoid them.

Some are obvious – surely you would not be dumb enough to paint on blackface or slanted eyes for a party – but others may be unexpected.

For example, the expression "you people" is considered very offensive, even if it as used as part of a compliment, such as *You people have the very best restaurants. I love your food.*

And even though you might call your own beloved Danish children your *abeunger*, American children should never be called monkeys for any reason, particularly dark-skinned American children.

What to do if you make a mistake

If you make a mistake, consider apologizing even if you secretly feel you were right or the other person is being too sensitive.

It is often worth it to maintain business and personal relationships, and to avoid having the offended person spreading the incident on traditional or social media.

Should the incident happen in a professional setting, it might be worth consulting your lawyer or HR people to make sure the episode has been entirely put behind you.

Religion and what it means for your business

Danes see the US as extremely religious, and in some ways it is.

The first European settlers to the US were religious refugees, and religion was a factor in many of the most important American historical events, including the civil rights movement lead by Reverend Dr. Martin Luther King Jr.

Meanwhile, the current wave of immigration has made new Americans out of millions of Christians, Muslims, Buddhists, and Sikhs from Asia, Africa, and South America.

The continued (thrilling) uncertainty of life in the United States means many seek comfort and guidance from a higher power.

Part of daily life

Americans have the ability to integrate religion into almost any daily activity. You'll see American football players point up to the sky when they've made a big play (*God assisted them!*) or game show contestants asking for the Lord's help to win the big prize.

A business colleague may suggest a "come to Jesus" meeting when it's time to have a frank talk with an underperforming supplier. And in a social setting, if a friend is cheerfully misbehaving, someone may say jokingly, *Y'all need Jesus!*

On the other hand, fewer and fewer Americans attend church every Sunday or are members of an established church at all.

The churches that still pull in worshippers tend to be showbiz-style megachurches, arena-size gatherings with rock n' roll choirs and impressive light shows.

Don't look down your nose at religion

Many Danes are atheists or agnostics (despite the big Christian cross on their flag), and some look down on religious people. "It's foolish. It's like believing in ghosts," one Dane told me.

Believe what you want, but it's a good idea to hide your contempt from believers who may be your business partners or employees.

It's also important to treat everyone equally. If you let Employee A print out fliers for her church open house using the office color printer, make sure you also let Employee B print out fliers for his mosque open house using the same color printer.

Religious stereotypes

"Religious" means different things to different people, so don't assume that because someone calls themselves religious that they do not drink alcohol, will get upset at salty language, or are uncomfortable with gay or transgender people. (Some churches are explicitly LGBTQ-friendly.)

For many people, especially new immigrants, a church, mosque, or Hindu temple is the place where they meet up with family and friends, stage holiday dinners, and relax and enjoy life.

It's somewhat the equivalent of a Danish local football association.

Long working hours and the persistence of stay-at-home parents

Stuck in the office until all hours, your American colleagues will no doubt comment on the short Danish workdays. "If I call at four o'clock your time, everyone has already gone home," they may complain.

This is true: Danes value their free time, and Danish bosses do not expect their employees to show "team spirit" by staying at the office into the evening, as US managers often do.

On the other hand, Danish employees are expected to focus exclusively on the work at hand during their office hours.

There are no extra-long lunches, taking a half-hour off

to pick up dry-cleaning, or using the company's secure IT network to send Grandma flowers on her birthday – all infractions which I have personally committed while working in the US.

When I worked on Wall Street, we often racked up 12 hour days, but those extra hours were not exclusively productive work.

Beating the system

Unlike Danish employees, American employees often feel like they are being monitored. (Sometimes they are.)

That means they may use various tricks to beat the system. For example, one of my Danish customers complained that her American colleagues wouldn't provide a shared view of their calendars.

This drove the Danes crazy, since it was impossible to schedule phone meetings without a clear view of when everyone was available.

But the Americans didn't want anyone to know they were taking an hour off here and there to take the car in for servicing, or to see their kids' school theater productions.

They felt justified in balancing their overtime with unscheduled time off (*I worked last weekend, so I'm taking a couple of hours now!*) but not justified enough to try to explain it to their Danish bosses.

If you decide to do it the Danish way in your office, make sure to explain that Danish-style limited office hours mean a complete focus on work while in the office.

And then set the example yourself.

The stay-at-home parent

Long working hours is one of the reasons why having a full-time stay-at-home parent is still a popular option for well-off American families. In fact, having the income to allow one parent to concentrate full-time on domestic engineering is a bit of a status symbol.

Given the high cost of day care in the US and the necessity of driving children everywhere until they turn 16, staying home can also make practical economic sense for the family.

Company parties in the US generally include your colleagues' significant others, so if you are introduced to one of these stay-at-home parents there's no reason to assume he or she is a 1950s-style housewife.

Many stay-at-homes have university degrees and choose to set aside good careers to focus on raising a family, particularly while their children are small. Some have side hustles, like a cupcake business or a YouTube channel.

Others provide for their child's entire education at home, usually because they don't trust the public school system.

There are so many of these "home schooled" kids in the US that they have their own sports leagues to provide exercise and the competitive experience that is so important to Americans.

Politeness and profanity

Danish children, and some Danish adults, tend to think English-language profanity is cute.

They drop words like *fuck* and *shit* into everyday conversations at times when they would never use their Danish equivalents.

This is a no-no in an American business context, where these words are as offensive as *slik mig i røven!* might be in a Danish business context.

So are religious exclamations like *Jesus!* in areas where people might use that word as an opening of a prayer.

Avoid racial and gender slurs

If you're a fan of edgy TV shows or rap music, you've probably heard plenty of rough American English words to describe specific gender or ethnic groups.

The unwritten rule is that people within these groups are allowed to use them (for example, a group of lesbian motorcyclists can call themselves *Dykes on Bikes*), but people outside the group are punished severely if they do.

Don't risk it: the fallout, particularly on social media, can be severe.

The "n-word", despite its frequent use in Black popular culture, should be avoided entirely. Don't even sing along to a song containing the word. Hum if necessary.

How do I know the right word to use?

If you are describing a subgroup of Americans – say, a type of customers who might be interested in your product – but you aren't sure what the currently acceptable word for that group might be, there is an easy fix.

Check out a recent edition of the *New York Times* or the *Washington Post* and see what word or words they use to describe that group.

That term may not be perfect, but it will also not be so offensive that it could affect your business.

Why American employees won't go outside their job descriptions

I had just locked the door of my home in Copenhagen and was hurrying towards the bus stop when I got a call from a package deliveryman.

He had a dozen copies of my previous book, *How to Work in Denmark*, to deliver to me. Was I at home to accept them?

I told him that unfortunately I was just leaving and had a bus to catch.

"Wait at home for a couple more minutes," he said. "I'll make the delivery, and then I'll drive you to the bus stop."

Flexibility and initiative

It all worked out well. As it happened, the delivery driver had spent a lot of time in Alaska where he had worked with Inuit musicians, so we had a good chat in the cab of his truck. But I was even more impressed with his flexibility and initiative.

Danes are brought up to take charge of their work areas, and make the decisions necessary to get the job done.

Americans aren't always able do this, mostly for legal reasons. An American driver would be acutely aware that she was only insured to carry books, not authors, and that going outside her job description would be a risk to both herself and her company.

General vs specific instructions

In general, the unwillingness of Americans to go outside the strict guidelines of their job description can be frustrating to the Danes who manage them.

Danes want to give general instructions – *paint me a picture of a forest* – and rely on the employee's expertise to fill in the rest and deliver it by deadline.

But American employees are accustomed to more specific instructions. *Paint me a picture of a forest in winter, with three large trees, two deer, and a hunter.* And they also expect more monitoring and milestones. *Show me the first version by Tuesday, and the finished product by Friday.*

Why you may need more managers

The Danish way is to simply trust that the people who report to you are doing their jobs right.

But in the US, you as a manager are professionally, personally, and legally responsible for making sure your employees are doing their jobs right, and for painstakingly tracking and recording them so they can be dismissed if they aren't.

If you don't have time for all this, you might have to hire someone who does, which is why American companies often have more layers of management than Danish ones do.

"My door is always open"

One of the expressions Danish managers like best is, *My door is always open.*

What they mean by this is multi-layered. On one hand, they want to seem approachable, as opposed to a distant, iron-handed supervisor.

But wrapped up in that accessibility is also a quiet demand: *I want you to come to me as quickly as possible if something is wrong.*

If a project is late, if you've discovered a mistake, if you are not getting along with a colleague, come to me proactively and let me know. My door is open and I am waiting.

Your American employees may not hear *my door is always open* with those same layers of meaning.

To them, you sound friendly and perhaps ready to "shoot the breeze" during working hours chatting about topics of light interest, like sports.

Don't expect proactive information

Coming to you with a difficult issue, particularly if it does not concern their specific job description, may seem like unnecessarily asking for trouble.

This is particularly true if they would have to go over the head of their direct boss in order to speak with you. That would be seen as deeply disloyal and a little sneaky.

And if it's a colleague they are having a problem with – and that person is in one of the protected classes – employees may worry they will be accused of bigotry.

Instead, they may find it easier to simply let the problem fester. "Stay in your lane," is a currently popular expression, a modern update of "mind your own business".

Alternately, they may take the problem to someone whose job description involves dealing with it, such as your HR team. In the worse-case scenario, they may even approach some outside actor, like a regulatory agency or the media.

I have no tips for you on how to get American employees to act like Danish ones when it comes to sharing information upwards.

But be aware that the informal, employee-initiated conversations you expect in Denmark are less likely to happen in the US.

Leveraging the American love of sports and competition

After learning English, learning the language of sports is the next best way to fit into US culture, and it is a great source of easy small talk for business.

Basketball, American football, and baseball are the three most important sports, although figure skating and swimming are popular topics of discussion when the Olympics roll around.

The sports you follow for business reasons will depend on the location of the people you do business with.

Wisconsin, for example, is totally enamored of its football team, the Green Bay Packers. New York City is more of a baseball town, with two teams, the historic New

York Yankees and the newer New York Mets.

Detroit goes for hockey and Seattle likes soccer. Los Angeles lives and breathes for the Lakers basketball team.

College sports are important too

Those are professional teams, but in many locations, particularly in the South, the local university (or "college") team is more important.

College sports are seen as somewhat more authentic than professional ones, since the players are all young strivers who don't display the boredom or arrogance of their multimillionaire professional counterparts.

During March of each year, offices all over the US engage in "March Madness", when they try to predict the winner of the annual NCAA college basketball championship. An elaborate bracket system and minor gambling is usually involved.

(For a thoroughly American experience, attend a college football game if you can get tickets. Historically black American colleges are particularly well-known for their excellent marching bands and creative cheerleading squads.)

How you can use US sports in business

Ask an important business contact which team he follows, and then put a memo on your calendar to do a deep-dive into the team's recent progress before your next meeting.

Just being able to ask the right questions (*Any chance they'll make the playoffs? They're in a tough division this year*) will warm up the sports fan and pave the way for successful business to be accomplished.

One of my Danish customers had telephone meetings every Monday with a team in Minnesota. Setting up Google Alerts meant the Danish colleagues were able to start every conversation (at least in football season) with an opener like, *Wow, what a game on Sunday. The Vikings really turned it around in the final quarter, didn't they?*

The American colleagues were happy to share the joy of victory, or appreciated the sympathy when the Vikings were defeated. The meetings went well.

Bring sports to your company

Many companies field their own sports teams, usually low-impact sports like softball and bowling. This is more about socializing with each other and with people in the industry than it is about serious competition.

That said, Americans love to compete, and you can introduce some of the thrill of the game with small contests and incentive programs in the office.

Who can come up with the best name for our fall party? Which team can achieve the cleanest desks before the Labor Day break? Which call center specialist will have the best customer satisfaction rating for March?

The prize can be something as simple as a $25 gift card towards a meal at a local restaurant, but your American colleagues will still enjoy playing to win.

Meetings and negotiations with US business partners

A slightly shocked Danish businessman was telling me about a sales meeting he'd recently had with an American company.

"Before the meeting they were all friendly and joking," he said.

"Then once it started, they were like sharks. They wanted a better price and a faster delivery schedule than we'd anticipated, and they wanted us to make a commitment right away. We felt like we'd been clobbered."

"Once the meeting was over they went back to being friendly and joking again, as if nothing had happened."

Aggression and emotion

This isn't unusual in US business culture. *Small talk is all well and good, but time is money and when it comes to business, we're here to get stuff done.*

Danes will probably appreciate this directness. They also like to get to the point quickly, but they may not be prepared for the aggression and emotion that can be part of negotiations in the US.

In particular, as a meeting reaches its crescendo and an agreement is tantalizingly near, the drama can increase. Confrontation is likely. Harsh truths may be spoken. Will the deal get done?

This is not the time to play the controlled, cold-blooded Dane with to-be-or-not-to-be detachment.

Show that you are as enthusiastic about the possibilities of this business as the Americans are – within the limits of your own profitability, of course.

Drama just means the Americans are sincerely interested.

Be prepared to think big

One mistake Danes make in meetings is being too focused on the matter at hand.

They're very well prepared for what's on the agenda (no need to call the home office in Denmark, where people have probably gone home anyway because of the time

difference) and have a solid plan for a specific deal.

But their American counterparts may not want to limit themselves to that specific deal. They may think *bigger, bigger, bigger!* Maybe there could be a much wider palette of cooperation between our companies. Maybe there is so much more business opportunity than we'd ever imagined.

In American business – as in American life – you can always go much lower or much higher, in price or in scope. Negotiations with Americans may be more organic. *What about if we do* **this***?*

Be prepared for a freeform discussion, and keep in mind that US business people are more open to up-selling than their Danish counterparts might be.

Transparency and trust

Denmark is a culture based on trust and transparency, and Danes sometimes take that transparency into their business negotiations.

Look, they may say, *this is how much we are paying for the product or our vendors*, perhaps even showing itemized lists of expenses.

The Americans don't expect this and don't really want this. A lump sum price will do just fine, thank you. And on the other side of the table, they have no intention of showing you an itemized list of *their* expenses.

Does the price work for you? Great, then let's go.

Cementing a deal

When negotiations are over, trusting Danes often rely on a handshake agreement and go home believing a deal has been done.

But for Americans, the handshake is only the first step, and a letter or email outlining the agreement the second.

The deal isn't really done until lawyers have drawn up a fat contract the size of a Danish-English dictionary, both sides' legal teams have carefully reviewed it (never skip this part of the process), and the contract is finally signed.

Reverence for the military

For a largely pacifist country like Denmark, the American reverence for the military and the people who serve in it can come as a surprise.

But it can be difficult to avoid. Anyone in a uniform, or who used to be in a uniform, is seen as deserving of respect in the US. This can even be true for antiwar types, who protest the wars the US military are sent to fight but respect the individuals who fight them.

It helps that the military is seen as a good way for non-white Americans to advance to managerial positions on a merit-only basis.

"Thank you for your service"

If a member of the military is in uniform and dines in a restaurant, he or she will often find their bill has been paid

for them by an anonymous donor who writes "Thank you for your service" on the settled bill.

Giving up your business-class airplane seat so a uniformed member of the military won't have to fly sardine class is also considered good manners; former members of the military often do this for current service members.

Many US politicians, male and female, are military veterans, including some with visible war injuries like lost legs or eyes.

What this means to you as a business person

It's common for US companies to offer discounts to active service members or military veterans. Some of your customers may ask for one.

When hiring, many businesses see military service (with an honorable discharge) as a strong positive.

Basically, the US government has already done your management training for you. Veterans are people who have been taught leadership and goal-fulfillment under the most trying of circumstances.

Different health insurance needs

Military veterans and their families may also have different health insurance needs than your other employees, since veterans have a right to tax-funded health care for the rest of their lives.

Unfortunately, the Veterans Administration is one of the many federal government agencies known for corruption and negligence, which is why you will also see homeless people in America with cardboard signs saying they are veterans struggling with mental illness, addiction, or both.

The poor performance of the Veterans Administration health infrastructure is one of the reasons many Americans are cynical about government-run health care.

Humility, self-irony, Danish humor and why you should avoid all three

Good character, in Danish eyes, requires a great deal of humility. *Du skal ikke tro, at du er noget.* Danes are raised to be modest about their personal contributions, even as they show pride in the fine products they produce.

This works great in Denmark, but it is lost on the Americans, who see good character as confidence, friendliness, and an ability to fix things that are broken.

If you downplay your own skills – or even worse, your product – they will take that at face value and assume you are a loser who doesn't have much to offer.

Discarding a lifetime of learned modesty

If you are going to succeed in business in the US, you will have to put aside a lifetime of learned modesty and

start convincingly telling people that your product is very good indeed, and that their personal or business lives will be much improved if they purchase it.

Americans are used to these passionate sales pitches and won't be offended by them as long as your claims are true.

In my communications consulting business in Denmark, I once worked with a customer who wrote in Danish that his company *har haft held og dygtighed til at udvikle et system der i al beskedenhed ikke findes sikrere på markedet.*

The direct translation, "We had the luck and talent to develop a system that in all modesty cannot be found in a more secure form on the market," would have sounded ludicrous to his American audience.

I translated it to read "We developed one of the most secure systems on the market."

"Self-irony" is not a word

Another challenge for Danes doing business in the US is that Danish humor simply doesn't translate there.

Self-irony is neither a real word in American English (use "self-mocking humor" instead) nor a common concept in the United States.

Irony, the cultural anthropologists tell us, works best in a situation where everyone has a long shared history and

common points of reference – like Denmark.

For this reason, Carlsberg never ran its famous "Probably the best beer in the world" advertising campaign in the US.

Probably the best beer? the Americans would have thought. *Why not just bring me the best beer?*

Watch out for sarcasm

Many Danes are fond of sarcasm, which they believe shows intelligence.

Occasionally they even use it passive aggressively. "Great cleaning," I saw written in a cloud of dust on a mirror at my Danish fitness center. (*"Do they mean that backwards?"* the puzzled Nigerian cleaning man asked me.)

In the US, like Nigeria, sarcasm is likely to be misunderstood, or at least not appreciated.

It could gain you a reputation as a "negative person", which is one of the worst things you can be from an American point of view.

Why positive feedback is so important for your business

One of the most persistent complaints I hear from Americans working for or with Danes is the lack of positive reinforcement.

"We only hear from them when something is wrong," they say.

From the Danish point of view, this makes perfect sense. *We hired you to do a job, you're doing it, and we'll let you know if there is a problem.*

But for Americans who grow up in a culture of constant positive reinforcement, this can come off as grouchy and unsupportive.

Jantelov and Grundtvig

For Danes, this approach has its roots in a combination of *Jantelov* and the Grundtvig teachings that form the basis of the Danish educational system.

Jantlov teaches Danes not to brag too much, and Grundtvig schooling brings them up to believe that they can get that magic 13 grade (at least back in the day) if they are clever enough to teach the teacher something new.

The result is a Danish boss who can look at a project that is 98% right and feel like he's added value by pointing out the 2% that is wrong.

This is a recipe for demoralized American employees.

The sandwich method

Most US business students are taught "the sandwich method" of praise and criticism, and even those not specifically trained in it will recognize it immediately.

The trick is to build up goodwill by repeated praise that creates a flowering meadow of employee confidence, so that the occasional weed you point out can be removed quickly and with a smile.

So American bosses start with a bit of fluffy praise (*"You've worked so hard on this. Thanks for your extra effort"*), followed by some meat (*"I'm not sure if your conclusion holds, though, given the labor costs involved"*), followed by some more praise (*"I do appreciate your ability to think outside the*

box, however. Always feel free to come to me with suggestions like this.")

A waste of time? Maybe. But it is what your American team is expecting.

Without the cushion built up by positive feedback, even legitimate criticism can let the air out of their balloon entirely.

That can mean low employee engagement, poor workplace satisfaction, and even the departure of valued employees.

Convenience and why a lack of it could torpedo your business in the US

It could happen to you: you enter a large American supermarket, walk what seems to be several kilometers as you fill your cart, and as you pay at the cash register you see a man *stealing your food.* There he is, putting everything you have just purchased into his bag!

Except he's not a thief: he's an employee of the grocery store, a "bagger." This employee, often a local teenager, new immigrant, or person with an intellectual disability, will pack everything nicely into bags and then put the bags in your cart so that all you need to do is roll it to your car.

This is convenience, American-style.

Customer convenience is paramount

One of the aspects of American life that Danish businesspeople often struggle with is the American love of convenience.

Whether you are B2C or B2B, you will be expected to structure your business around your customers' convenience – and not, unfortunately, around the mental health of your employees.

American employees are expected to be accessible to their customers at any time during working hours (unless they are in a meeting) and sometimes outside of working hours too.

The concept of a "telephone time" – a specified two or three hours per day when an employee at the doctor's office, tax authority, or fitness center is willing to pick up the telephone – was something I never experienced before I moved to Denmark.

Don't try this in the US, where the customer is king.

Make it easy to be your customer

Making life easier for your customers is crucial for doing business in the US. Learning about, purchasing, using, and re-purchasing your product should be as easy as possible.

If you don't make it easy, one of your competitors will, and your customer may not give you a second chance.

Perhaps your employees are so busy that they don't have time to immediately respond to customers. In that case, hire more employees.

Americans and vacation time: Two weeks and they don't take it all?

While Americans don't envy everything about the Danish system (at least not as much as Danes like to believe they do), they do envy the amount of vacation time Danes receive by law.

US federal law does not mandate any paid vacation or holidays, and up to 25% of employees, mostly low-wage and part-time workers, don't get any at all.

The average for employees at private companies is about 16 days per year, which increases with seniority to a maximum of 25 days per year.

Three-day weekends are popular

This is why "three-day weekends" are popular. Almost all of the US national holidays are scheduled on a Monday,

so that people can get away to visit family and friends.

Some people extend the holiday by a day or two, so scheduling an important project deadline on the Friday before or the Tuesday after one of these holidays is a bad idea.

You may also want to avoid business or personal travel at these times or around Thanksgiving weekend in November, because airports and highways can be extremely busy.

(Unlike their Danish counterparts, American shops are open on these national holidays, and may even run special sales. It can be disconcerting to see a car dealer offer *low! low! low!* prices for a holiday like Memorial Day, which honors dead US soldiers.)

Longer vacations

When one of your employees takes a longer vacation, it is usually for one week, and he often visits family elsewhere in the US or takes his kids to a big amusement park like Disney World or to the country-music mecca of Branson, Missouri. Singles might take a city trip with friends, or make plans to run a marathon or see a show elsewhere in the country.

Two-week vacations are unusual, and are usually reserved for honeymoons.

Three- or four-week vacations are seen as a crazy indulgence or perhaps the sign of a mental breakdown that needs healing before the employee can get back to work.

I remember when I first came to Denmark how surprised I was at the standard summer question, "Are you taking three or four?"

Should you offer Danish vacations?

If for some reason your company is able to offer Danish-level vacations to American employees, that could be a very strong competitive edge when it comes to recruiting.

But keep in mind that in the US the customer's needs come first, not the employee's.

Your US customers will not be happy to find out that their trusted contact has taken off on what sounds to them like an infinite holiday.

The idea that some customer need should remain unfulfilled for a week or two because an employee is relaxing is totally foreign to the American marketplace, and it is a good way to lose business. *The customer comes first.*

Why Americans don't take all their vacation

This focus on customer satisfaction is one of the reasons that Americans often don't take all the vacation they're entitled to.

There is also a certain pressure to be seen at work, to be seen as necessary and vital to the company's operations. *If they realize that my department runs well without me, maybe they'll realize that they don't need me.*

This fear is also why Americans are much more likely than their Danish counterparts to take phone calls and answer emails when they are supposedly on holiday.

(And why they will be frustrated when their Danish counterparts totally disappear and go *incommunicado* during their own vacations.)

No trips to Europe

Incidentally, these short vacation allowances are a good reason why Danes should not get on their high horses about Americans having seen so few places in Europe.

A flight to a Swiss ski resort that takes two hours from Copenhagen takes 12 hours from San Diego. That cuts two days out of a one-week vacation, not accounting for jet lag.

It's much more efficient to go skiing in Utah, which is a two-hour flight.

What to do if you're stopped by an American cop

Law enforcement is much more a part of daily life in US than it is in Denmark. You're more likely to see cops and more likely to come in contact with them.

There are so many different types of cops – city cops, county sheriff's office, state highway patrol, even federal investigators like the FBI – that it can take a moment to figure out who is stopping you and why.

Most cops are fine people, just doing a job and trying to get home to their families in one piece, but there are unfortunately a few bad eggs, and you never know when you're going to get one.

What to do if you're stopped

If you're stopped by a law enforcement officer, keep your cool and be extremely polite – a "sir" or a "ma'am"

will come in handy. Pleasant and professional is the best tone to take.

Keep your hands in view at all times so the officer has no reason to believe you're reaching for a weapon.

Answer the officer's basic questions with a smile, but don't submit to unreasonable requests either.

Orders versus requests

An officer may *order* you to do something like show your driver's license or get out of the car, but if an officer *asks permission* to do something – *"May I search your car?"* – you are in your rights to politely say no.

You never know how you might unintentionally be breaking a law: an open bottle of liquor anywhere in a car, even in the trunk, is a crime in some states. Anyway, the cop is not looking for evidence to prove your innocence. She is looking for evidence of a possible crime.

If the officer really needs to search that car, she will get a warrant from a judge to do so, usually by telephone.

"Am I under arrest?" you can ask the police officer if she has kept you waiting for a while. "Or am I free to go?"

What to do if you're arrested

If you are arrested, it's time to stop talking. You really do have the right to remain silent, just like they say in the movies.

Name, address, and possibly your nationality is all you need to disclose before you call your lawyer, your consulate or both.

Don't get nervous and don't start blathering and possibly get yourself into even more trouble.

Whatever dumb thing you say can be used against you in a court of law – just like in the movies.

Speeding tickets

There's an unwritten rule that you can generally go 5-10 miles above the speed limit on highways and not get a ticket.

But it's also true that some municipalities use speeding tickets as a revenue source and will happily stop cars with out-of-state license plates to collect whatever they can.

If you live nearby, you can opt to go to the local court and challenge a speeding ticket.

If you don't live nearby, you're probably stuck paying. Unpaid speeding tickets can end up attached to your name online and come up when people Google you, assuming the arresting officer can spell your Danish name correctly.

Alternately, they can just sit there acquiring interest and penalties until you get stopped again in the US and end up paying for two tickets or more.

Don't be Karl Smart

Danish authorities generally have a sense of humor, traceable to the *Jantelov* mockery directed at anyone being foolish enough to think they are in a position of authority in the first place.

American authorities do not have a sense of humor. Do not joke with them, ever, about possible crimes you have committed or possible contraband you may be carrying. They are legally obliged to take every statement seriously.

A fellow cultural trainer once told me about a gig he'd had with a company that had experienced difficulty sending mechanics to fix windmills the US.

The mechanics, working class Danish good ol' boys, would bristle at the US immigration officers' routine questions about whether they were potential communists or terrorists.

"Yes, I am a terrorist!" the Karl Smarts from Brøndby or Randers would say. "I'm here to blow you all up!"

At which time they were immediately sent back to Denmark.

The cultural trainer made a good bit of income training the mechanics to answer such questions with a "no" and a stiff smile, so the windmills could actually get fixed.

Guns and violent crime

The vast majority of violent crime in the US takes place between people who know each other, often people who have been engaged in some kind of criminal enterprise with each other.

Mass shootings do take place, but the number of people killed by them in the vast US each year is only double the number of people who drown in tiny Denmark (roughly 125 mass shooting deaths to 59 drownings.)

If you are worried about violence, don't buy illegal drugs or attempt poverty tourism in the worst parts of town, and you are likely to be fine.

Not getting "Danish drunk" and wandering around unfamiliar cities in the middle of the night will help too.

Why many Americans don't trust their own government

The Danish government is imperfect, and the headlines tell us every day about the ways it has fallen short.

Still, most Danes have a basic faith that their government is mostly good and reflects what the people of Denmark desire. This is one reason they are willing to share so much of their income with the tax authorities.

Many Americans do not have this basic faith in government, particularly the federal government in Washington, and you will find it reflected in your daily business conversations.

Everyone wants something different

In a multicultural country like the United States, everyone wants something slightly different from their government.

People on the right want strong law-and-order provisions that arrest crooks and keep them in jail. People on the left want the federal government to stand for social justice, protecting and elevating vulnerable groups.

And both sides want to enjoy benefits like old-age pensions, disability allowances, college tuition support, and federal highways while paying the least possible amount of taxes for them.

This eagerness to get stuff without paying for it means the federal government tends to overpromise and underdeliver, along with running up enormous deficits.

Rules that may or may not be enforced

In business, you'll find that this results in a large number of federal regulations that may or may not be useful and may or may not be enforced, depending on the situation.

(This is in addition to state, city, and county rules, plus in some places water district and school district rules.)

Dealing with the federal government can also be a trip back in time, with paper forms and online interfaces that seem to have been designed during Bill Clinton's administration (1993-2001).

If you haven't written a check in 20 years, or you are a young person who has never written a check, dealing with the US federal government may give you that opportunity.

A headache or a hinderance

Part of the problem is that Washington, DC, which was chosen to be at the center of a young country in 1790, is now a long distance from much of the country, both geographically and culturally.

A recent survey found that only 11% of Americans found Congress, the US version of the *Folketing*, to be trustworthy. (The most trusted institution was the military, at 74%.)

In business, "Washington" is almost always spoken about in tones of a headache or a hinderance – unless the federal government is a customer, and then your government contacts and their large open wallets are spoken about glowingly.

Beware of federal law enforcement

One part of the federal government that does tend to work very well is law enforcement.

Should you hear that the Federal Bureau of Investigation (FBI), the SEC (Securities and Exchange Commission), or the Internal Revenue Service (IRS) is investigating you, your company, or your industry, this is something to be very worried about indeed.

Federal law enforcement has the reputation of being highly efficient, draconian, and unforgiving.

Fear and the American employee

There are many books on managing Americans that are more comprehensive than this one, but few seem to touch on one of the primary motivators of the American worker, which is fear.

Danes who have always lived with the comforting arms of the welfare state ready to catch them if they fall can have a hard time understanding people who have almost no safety net at all.

An American who loses her job can lose her health insurance, her home, her car, her kids' college fund, and even her marriage, not to mention her identity in a culture that promotes self-definition through work.

Someone with so little backup will behave very

differently at work than an employee who has *dagpenge* and the coaches at the *A-kasse* to tide her over for a couple of years.

Fear and the management relationship

In particular, this background of fear affects employees' relationships with their bosses. Because a boss can make hiring and firing decisions, she has an enormous amount of power over their lives.

Danish bosses who show up in the US expecting to have the "eye level" relationship with their team that they're accustomed to in Denmark will be disappointed.

American employees aren't likely to contradict their boss or tell her if she's making a mistake. They may ask some pointed questions, but if the boss insists on a course of action they may just shrug their shoulders and follow along.

"Well, she's the boss," they say and do as commanded, while silently polishing their cv's.

Fear and work habits

Fear is also the reason Americans do their best to look busy, busy, busy on the job.

They feel they need to justify their paychecks, and avoid being seen as "dead wood" that can be dispensed with in the next round of layoffs.

When I first arrived in Denmark, after a decade of working in the hyper-competitive environment of Manhattan, I brought my American habits of performative busyness with me.

That meant I stupidly avoided taking a few minutes off to join my colleagues for the celebratory cake that goes along with new babies, new jobs, and upcoming vacations. Too busy! Too busy!

It took me a while to figure out that this was counterproductive, and that stopping to join my colleagues for cake was in fact *part of the job*. It helped create office friendships and solidarity.

If you want your American employees to join you for cake, cloak it as part of a required meeting so they don't feel guilty about it.

(And don't forget to cater to the employees who are vegan, gluten-free, lactose-intolerant, kosher, halal, or otherwise on restricted diets. Fruit plate, anyone?)

Charities and how to contribute without getting in trouble

If you establish an office in the US, local charities will begin to approach you for donations and sponsorships.

Contributing to community organizations is a great way to give back to the community, as well as build your local profile.

That said, choosing the right charity is important, because choosing the wrong charity can prove to be a substantial business negative.

The case of Chick-fil-A

If you follow American business, you may have heard the story of Chick-fil-A, a national chicken sandwich chain with a reputation for excellent service and for treating its employees well.

Chick-fil-A is owned by an evangelical Christian and is closed on Sundays. In the past it made charitable donations to Christian organizations like the Fellowship of Christian Athletes, which excludes gays and lesbians.

For this reason, the chicken chain has faced ongoing boycotts by LGBTQ groups and has been prohibited by law from opening in some locations.

Research before you give

The lesson: don't give to any charity before you've thoroughly researched it and found out if there is any opposition to it in your community.

It's also a good idea to check how much of what the charity collects goes to its cause and how much of it goes to administrators. Charity financial records are public; a search on "Charity Navigator" will help you examine them.

Beware of political giving

Be particularly careful if you are approached by political candidates in the US.

All donations to candidates are public and there are very specific laws about what non-US companies or non-citizens can contribute.

"If you can walk, you can work": Health and health insurance in the US

You've no doubt heard plenty of horror stories about the US health system, and there are plenty to go around.

The administrative burden is unbelievable, with enough forms filled out every year to wallpaper the Atlantic Ocean.

And the payment system is totally out of whack, with privately insured patients being charged absurd amounts to cover providers for the expense of uninsured patients who cannot pay their bills.

What does it mean for you as a Dane working or doing business in the US?

Go nowhere without health insurance

First of all, make sure you have health insurance before

you ever set foot in the US, and make sure that insurance covers business trips and not just personal ones.

If you are unlucky enough to have a serious incident like a car accident, the paramedics will not leave you at the roadside bleeding without proof of insurance, but someone at the hospital will ask you for it – and probably ask you to fill out some forms – as soon as you are conscious.

You will be running up some big bills for the care you receive, and you may receive excessive care, as the medical professionals around you practice "defensive medicine", putting you through every possible test and procedure to avoid a malpractice lawsuit at a later date.

(Always examine your US medical bills, and challenge them if you think they are ridiculous, which they often are.)

Luxury health care in a for-profit market

One aspect that goes unsaid in the great health care debate is that US healthcare is not only excellent for those who can afford to pay, it goes beyond excellent, which means it will make up or at least over-diagnose syndromes for its most profitable clients.

Most well-off Americans get an "annual physical", a kind of all-around checkup that sends them home with a list of numbers describing their blood pressure, cholesterol levels, blood sugar, and body-mass index, all of which they can quote at a moment's notice. (Don't *ask* them about

their numbers though; this violates privacy laws.)

American television is full of ads selling expensive drugs that viewers are encouraged to "ask their doctor" about, and elaborate medical equipment is marketed to well-insured customers as well.

An American friend recently disclosed on Facebook that almost everyone in his circle had a CPAP hood for sleep apnea. These frightening-looking hoods cost up to $3000, paid for by insurance if you have it.

Minor complaints and little illnesses

Should you have a minor complaint while in the US, like an ear infection or a troubled stomach, chain stores like CVS and Walmart have walk-in clinics in some locations. A nurse practitioner will see you for a small fee and might even do a lab test or write a prescription.

Most of these stores also have pharmacists that can direct you to the right over-the-counter medicine for a hacking cough, menstrual cramps, or other everyday maladies.

No time off to drink tea

While the traditional Danish approach to small problems like this is to relax, drink tea, and take time off until you feel better, this will not be appreciated in the US.

First of all, most companies offer employees a limited number of sick days, and they are supposed to be used for

when you are entirely helpless. "If you can walk, you can work," is the usual American mantra.

For anything less than near-total immobility, you are expected to dope yourself up with over-the-counter pills so you can meet your obligations to your team and your customers.

Health insurance as an employee benefit

Most Americans get their health care through their employers. If you're hiring, offering a good health care plan is key to getting the right people.

Obamacare, the patchwork national health care plan put into place under US President Barack Obama, requires you to provide health care for all your employees once your American company reaches a certain size and your employees work a certain number of hours.

Consult your HR professional for the latest requirements, which change all the time. Your state and city location may also have specific legal requirements for employer-provided health care.

Privacy and employment

Health care privacy is a big deal in the US, and there are significant legal limits to what you can ask about the state of an employee's health.

If an employee's medical needs get in the way of doing the job they were hired to do, call a lawyer before you make any demands or terminate anyone's employment.

Keep in mind that alcoholism and drug abuse are also seen as medical problems, so if an employee is doing poorly because of substance abuse, you may need legal assistance before removing him from your team.

Making friends in the US, and why short-term friendships are OK

If you will be moving to the US or staying there for a few months at a time, you will probably want to build up a social life and make friends there.

Some Danes love the openness and congeniality of the Americans; how nice to be invited at the last minute to a relaxed family dinner that involves no tablecloths and no speeches.

Others find making friends with Americans frustrating, because the warmth sometimes displayed at a first meeting doesn't always develop into a long-term friendship.

One Danish businesswoman told me she'd been deeply disappointed by this.

"I met a woman through my yoga class, and she invited me over to dinner at her home, and I thought, *Great! I've*

made a friend," the Dane said. "But it never really turned into anything."

Deep friendships vs light friendships

Danes are known for their long and deep friendships, that frequently begin in childhood. A true friendship can endure for a lifetime, often outlasting marriages.

Americans have that type of friend too, but because they are always on the move (changing cities, changing neighborhoods, changing jobs) they also have short-term friendships.

These relationships can start at a dinner party, a networking event, or on a running team, and sometimes they progress to meeting for lunch, catching a movie, or going out for pizza. You might become best buddies, you might meet up for a beer once a month, or you might never see each other again.

Everybody's busy, and if you two don't head off into the sunset together it doesn't mean the relationship was superficial or meaningless. It was just short.

No iron curtain between work and free time

The iron curtain that divides work time from free time and colleagues from "private friends"* in Denmark doesn't exist in the US.

You and your colleagues may play golf or softball together on the weekend, or go out bowling or for drinks

after work on a Friday evening, perhaps to celebrate a birthday or a promotion.

When you're out on the town with your colleagues and you're in a loose group standing around a bar, it's considered perfectly good manners to begin chatting with other random people at the bar. Someone might strike up a conversation based on sports playing on the bar TV.

You might unexpectedly make a friend this way – or you might just go your separate ways after the game is over or the last drink is downed.

"Have a good one," you can say, and happily move on.

Making introductions

In Denmark, everyone is expected to stick out their hand and introduce themselves whenever new people enter the room.

But when you're in the US, you'll be expected to "perform the introductions" when bringing together two people who don't know each other.

In addition to stating their names and maybe where you know them from, it's also considered good manners to provide a little context and let the two know what they might have in common.

For example: *Sandra, this is Mike, who I know from my hiking club. Mike, Sandra is an old colleague from my time at*

IBM. I think you guys are actually both from the Pittsburgh area, right?

Now Mike and Sandra have something to talk about, and no one needs to feel isolated or ignored, except maybe you once Mike and Sandra begin what seems like an endless conversation about the Pittsburgh Steelers football team.

But at least you've helped two strangers become acquaintances, and maybe even friends.

Friendly interaction with strangers

In general, you'll have a lot more friendly interactions with strangers in the US than you do in Denmark, where people tend to walk around in a sealed bubble of privacy.

In the US it's not uncommon for a total stranger to give you a compliment, just for the sake of it, with no hidden agenda.

One Dane wrote online about an experience he'd had on a chilly day in New York City, when he went out wearing a colorful knit hat.

Across the street, a group of slightly tough-looking teenagers called out to him. "Cool hat, man!" they said. "Cool hat."

The Dane was a little worried. *Was this a trick? Were they planning to attack him?*

Nope. The teenagers just continued walking down the street, minding their own business.

They really did just like his hat.

Don't be the grumpy foreigner

On an online forum I frequent, one Danish businessman was asked what he thought of his time in America.

Ah, not too good, the man reported. *Houses are built flimsily. Cheeses and breads are essentially flavorless,* he said. *Mobile phone plans and broadband are too expensive. Bicycles there are considered sports equipment, not transportation devices. Strip malls are very unattractive. Breakfast products are mostly sugar. You can't really walk anywhere unless you are walking a dog.*

And most Americans he met agreed with his points, he added.

Sure buddy, I thought, they agreed *to your face.* As soon as you left the room they probably rolled their eyes and thought: there goes the grumpy foreigner.

The Yin and Yang of Janteloven

One of the great ironies of Danish culture is that while children are brought up to be modest about their personal qualities and achievements, they are also brought up to believe that Danish culture and Danish values are the best in the world.

With time and proper education, most Danes believe, everyone will share our values.

This reverse Janteloven really kicks into gear when Danes visit the US, which lacks many aspects of the welfare state that Danes are so proud of.

Danes feel a little sorry for the Americans for not having tax-funded health care, tax-funded universities, and a vast tax-funded social safety net to protect them against emergencies.

Built differently, operate differently

While many Americans would be happy to have these services, very few of them want to be taxed highly enough to pay for them, which is why the majority don't vote for politicians who would implement such programs.

The US is a high-risk, high-reward society; Denmark is a low-risk, egalitarian society. They're built differently, operate differently, and prioritize differently.

If you import to the US a condescending Danish-knows-best attitude, as well as complaints about the lack

of *rugbrød* and reliable bus service, you will annoy your business counterparts and become very unpopular.

A few tips on American English

Your English is probably fine for doing business with American colleagues, who are accustomed to hearing people speak with accents and make the occasional grammatical mistake.

Here, however, are some minor points of language that can trip up Danes.

(By the way, *amerikansk*, the Danish word for the language spoken in the US, is not translated directly. Most Americans will just say they speak *English*.)

* * *

In the US, the words *university* and *college* are used interchangeably when referring to undergraduate courses.

If a job applicant says he has just graduated from college,

he might have a degree from, say, New York University.

* * *

While the Danish word *velfærd* covers health care, education, and unemployment insurance, *welfare* in American English means income transfers to the nonworking poor, something a lot like *kontanthjælp*.

This is why your American colleagues may misunderstand your enthusiasm for the *velfærdsmodel*.

Those who are enthusiastic may not thoroughly grasp how high Danish taxes are in order to pay for *velfærd*; 44% of Americans pay no federal income tax at all.

* * *

At diskutere in Danish suggests that two parties disagree. That's not true of the verb "discuss" in English. A discussion is just a deeper, slightly more thoughtful version of a conversation. *Quibble* is a good English word to use for petty disagreements. *Stop quibbling!*

* * *

Såkaldt in Danish means that something has been given a name – *såkaldt babyboomgeneration*. But in American English, *so-called* almost always means it has been given a name it does not deserve. "That so-called mechanic destroyed my car's engine! "

* * *

Along the same lines, *kompetent* in Danish means quite capable, but *competent* in American English can be faint praise.

It often means effective but unspectacular, just barely good enough. "He's a competent actor – he shows up on time and knows his lines – but I wouldn't call him a star."

* * *

Thought-provoking in English is a positive thing, a bit like *tankevækkende* in Danish. It doesn't have the annoying undertone of *provokerende* in Danish.

* * *

Det interesserer mig ikke is an innocent way to shut down a boring conversation in Danish, but the English equivalent *I'm not interested* comes off as very harsh.

It's the sort of sharp dismissal used when a phone salesman calls you during dinner, or when an unappealing person makes repeated advances on you at a bar. *I'm not interested!*

If an American colleague begins to drone on about some personal interest you find irrelevant, a polite way to get out of it might be "*You know, that's not really my thing.*"

* * *

An *institution* in Danish can be a happy and positive place – a kindergarten, for example.

But in American English, a building that is an *institution*

is more often a place for severely disabled or deeply troubled people, like the criminally insane.

American colleagues may react with concern if you say that you are taking your child to an *institution*.

* * *

A kommode in Danish is a place to put your folded clothes. A *commode* in American English is a slang term for a toilet.

* * *

Speaking of toilets, if you need to empty your bladder after a long meeting and are seeking a place to do that, you'll find the Americans have many euphemisms for toilet facilities.

You can ask for the *restroom*, the *ladies' room* or the *men's room*, or the *bathroom*, even if you are in an office building and have no plans to take a bath.

Some women will still ask for the *powder room,* or say that they need to "*go powder their nose*" even though no one has carried around a powder puff for decades. Or they will say that need to "*freshen up.*"

Men might say they're headed for the "*little boy's room,*" that they plan to "*make a pit stop*" or even that they need to "*go see a man about a horse.*"

Just asking for *the toilet* is not wrong, but it's considered a bit explicit and vulgar.

The executive summary: Top things to remember

Thanks for reading this far in the book. Here are a few points to remember when doing business in the US.

- The US is a high-risk, high-reward climate. Relentless competition and potential failure is a feature, not a bug. Prepare to feel confused and unsafe. This means you're getting somewhere.

* * *

- The cool, controlled behavior that defines a mature adult in Denmark can make you seem uninterested or unmotivated in the US. Americans like to be fired up, and if you

want to do business with them you should be prepared to be just as enthusiastic.

* * *

- Cowboy image aside, Americans have much more respect for authority than the Danes. In a management or negotiation context, one boss makes the decision, for better or worse. Consensus is not required.

* * *

- Equal opportunity is a key aspect of the US legal system. Make sure your employees, suppliers, and customers are being treated equally regardless of their personal characteristics. Being able to prove that you have done this will, unfortunately, require more record-keeping than is usually done in Denmark.

* * *

- The sort of assumed trust that is possible in a monoculture like Denmark doesn't exist in the vast mosaic that is the US. Expect less transparency, and remember that the risk of litigation is on everyone's mind.

- You are expected to be available for your American customer almost all the time, and certainly within US working hours. Limited telephone times won't cut it, and customers won't be understanding if their valued contact disappears on a long Danish-style vacation.

* * *

- Danes tend to believe that their values and their system is the best in the world, which is understandable. But try to avoid sounding condescending because the US doesn't have this or that thing you are accustomed to at home. The US is a democracy, so if the majority of Americans wanted to pay for a Danish-style welfare state, they would have one. Not everyone wants to be Denmark.

* * *

- Enjoy the friendliness of Americans and their genuine interest in you and what you're up to, even if it isn't the beginning of a lifelong friendship. Relationships can be brief – sometimes very brief – and still have value.